PADDLE AND PUB

The best British pubs to get to by kayak, canoe or paddleboard

GEMMA BOWES

ADLARD COLES

LONDON · OXFORD · NEW YORK · NEW DELHI · SYDNEY

ADLARD COLES
Bloomsbury Publishing Plc
50 Bedford Square, London, WC1B 3DP, UK
Bloomsbury Publishing Ireland Limited
29 Earlsfort Terrace, Dublin 2, D02 AY28, Ireland

BLOOMSBURY, ADLARD COLES and the Adlard Coles logo
are trademarks of Bloomsbury Publishing Plc

First published in Great Britain 2025 • Copyright © Gemma Bowes, 2025

Gemma Bowes has asserted her right under the Copyright, Designs
and Patents Act, 1988, to be identified as Author of this work

All rights reserved. No part of this publication may be: i) reproduced or transmitted in any form, electronic or mechanical, including photocopying, recording or by means of any information storage or retrieval system without prior permission in writing from the publishers; or ii) used or reproduced in any way for the training, development or operation of artificial intelligence (AI) technologies, including generative AI technologies. The rights holders expressly reserve this publication from the text and data mining exception as per Article 4(3) of the Digital Single Market Directive (EU) 2019/790

A catalogue record for this book is available from the British Library

Library of Congress Cataloguing-in-Publication data has been applied for

ISBN: PB: 978-1-3994-1057-1; ePub: 978-1-3994-1056-4; ePDF: 978-1-3994-1055-7

2 4 6 8 10 9 7 5 3 1

Designed by Nicola Liddiard at Big Orange Door
Map illustrations by Louise Turpin
Bubbles motif by Alena Ohneva (iStock)
Photos on pages 51, 79, 107, 127, 149, 191, 211, 235 from iStock
Typeset in Poppins and New Kansas
Printed and bound in India by Replika Press

IMPORTANT SAFETY NOTICE AND LEGAL DISCLAIMER This book contains descriptions of paddling routes and locations around the UK. Undertaking any activity on or near water carries with it some risks that cannot be entirely eliminated, for example, you might get lost on a route or caught in bad weather. The information contained in this book should not be relied upon as a sole means of navigation. Users should consult all other relevant and available publications and information, such as the local Harbour Authority guidance or Waterway Authorities Navigation Notices. Users should also check local weather and water conditions with the appropriate authorities prior to departure.

The guidance contained in this book is based on the accumulated experience of the authors. Such guidance is generic and takes no account of users' own experience, advice from other paddlers, actual or forecast meteorological conditions, water conditions or other waterway users powered or otherwise.

All internet addresses given in this book were correct at the time of going to press. Bloomsbury Publishing Plc does not have any control over, or responsibility for, any third-party websites referred to or in this book.

The publishers and authors accept no responsibility for any errors or omissions, or for any accident, loss or damage arising from the misuse of information or guidance contained in this book.

Scotland

Northern Ireland

The Northwest

The Northeast

Wales

The Midlands

The East

The Southwest

The South

The Southeast

Contents

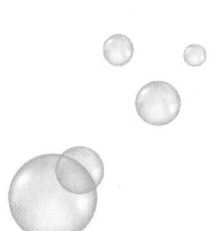

Introduction 6

The Southwest 13

1 St Agnes Heritage Coastline and The Driftwood Spars **14** • 2 River Telford and the Ferry Boat Inn **18** • 3 The Fal Estuary to the Pandora Inn **24** • 4 River Fowey: Fowey to Golant and Lerryn **28** • 5 Bigbury-on-Sea to Burgh Island **32** • 6 Salcombe Estuary: Kingsbridge to the Millbrook Inn **36** • 7 River Dart: Stoke Gabriel to the Maltsters Arms, Tuckenhay **40** • 8 Exeter Quay to the Double Locks Pub **44** • More great paddles in Devon **48**

The South 51

9 Christchurch and Avon Loop **52** • 10 Beaulieu River to the Yachtsman's Bar **56** • 11 River Hamble: Botley Brewery's Hidden Tap **60** • 12 Chichester Harbour: Itchenor to the Crown and Anchor **64** • 13 Basingstoke Canal: to Odiham's The Waterwitch **68** • 14 Upper Thames: Buscot to Lechlade **70** • More great paddles on the Upper Thames **74**

The Southeast 79

15 West London: Hurst Park to Richmond **80** • More great paddles in London **84** • 16 River Medway: from The Boathouse, Yalding **86** • 17 Wey Navigation: The Anchor **90** • 18 River Ouse: Barcombe Mills to The Anchor **94** • 19 River Cuckmere: Exceat to Seven Sisters **98** • 20 River Stour: Fordwich to Grove Ferry **102**

The East 107

21 Stour Valley: Sudbury to Bures **108** • 22 River Cam: Cambridge to Grantchester **112** • 23 Norfolk Rivers and Broads: River Waveney **118** • 24 Norfolk Rivers and Broads: Norwich and River Wensum **122**

The Midlands 127

25 Rivers Avon and Leam: Warwick to Leamington Spa **128** • 26 Kinver and the Staffordshire and Worcester Canal **132** • 27 River Severn: Bridgnorth to Arley **134** • 28 River Severn: Montford Bridge to Shrewsbury **138** • 29 Chester and the River Dee **144** • **More great paddles in the Midlands 147**

The Northeast 149

30 River Ouse: Bishopthorpe to Acaster Malbis **150** • 31 Staithes Harbour and the Cod and Lobster **154** • **More great paddles in North Yorkshire 158** • 32 River Tees: Stockton to Yarm **160** • 33 River Coquet: Amble to Warkworth **164** • 34 Beadnell Bay to Low Newton **168** • **More fishing villages on the Northumberland coast 171**

The Northwest 173

35 Lake District: Crummock Water and the Kirkstile Inn **174** • 36 Lake District: Bassenthwaite Lake **178** • 37 Lake District: Ullswater **182** • **More great paddles inthe Lake District 186** • **More great paddles in the Northwest 189**

Scotland 191

38 River Tweed: Peebles to Innerleithen **192** • 39 Argyll: Loch Sween and Tayvallich **196** • 40 Knoydart Peninsula and The Old Forge Inn **200** • 41 Highlands: Wester Ross and Applecross **204** • **More great paddles in Scotland 208**

Wales 211

42 Llyn Peninsula and the Ty Coch Inn **212** • 43 Llangollen Canal: Pontcysyllte Aqueduct **214** • 44 River Teifi: Cardigan and Cilgerran **218** • 45 River Wye: the 100-mile pub crawl **224** • 46 River Wye: Symonds Yat and Ye Old Ferrie Inn **230** • **More great paddles in Wales 233**

Northern Ireland 235

47 Causeway Coast: Ballycastle and the Giant's Causeway **236** • **More great paddles in Northern Ireland 238**

INTRODUCTION

The sun sparkles on the water as you ease your kayak or SUP in through gentle wash, paddle in hand, looking out to the start of your adventure. You are already feeling proud of yourself – you made it. You actually got out of the house and went down to the water, pumped up your vessel – or maybe hired a boat or finally booked that guided trip – and made the effort to do something different today. There's fun in store. The thrilling gliding feeling as you cut through the water, spray on your cheeks, nature all around, maybe a kingfisher or a seal to spot... and at the end, the promise of a lovely waterside pub, one of the country's true charmers. At some pretty, centuries-old tavern, you'll pull your vessel up onto the bank, squelch over to a sunny table and order your drink, a lovely ale, a crisp glass of wine, a cold pint or just a cracking cup of coffee. Then... relax.

That's the idea of this book; to get you back out there. Perhaps you've dabbled with paddling before; maybe that SUP you bought during lockdown isn't quite getting the use it once did and you need some motivation, or perhaps you're looking for new locations to kayak.

BELOW: Many of these paddles are suitable for the entire family – a lot of these pubs offer great food as well as tasty drinks.

The routes selected here are all, largely, about having a bit of fun. Most are easy going, or easy to cut short, and all end in a great riverside, lakeside, canalside or seaside drinking spot; some link several together.

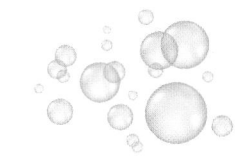

First things first, I want to make it very clear that paddling under the influence is a bad idea, as dangerous as drink-driving or drunk cycling. Save the booze for your post-paddle tipple, and stick to soft or hot drinks while en route. Maybe a half pint or very small cheeky one, especially if you're eating too (and there are some great foodie pubs featured), is something you can tolerate and still manage to paddle safely. I'll leave that up to you. But most of the operators featured in this book recommend not drinking at all while paddling – plenty of hire places and guided trips forbid it, in fact – so please be careful, and don't paddle pissed.

There's much to enjoy in these pubs anyway – fine food, centuries of history, lovely waterside beer gardens (where a good cup of tea can be just as enjoyable as a bottle). Some have stylish bedrooms to stay over in, so you can roll into bed without a care for the onward journey. Some of these pubs are great for cutting loose, where you can stay late and have a whale of a time, even if your trousers are wet and you smell like pond. I've given ideas for how to turn each trip into a weekend away, too.

The idea for this book came off the back of my own first pub paddle, some years ago on the River Fowey from Golant to the Ship Inn in Lerryn in Cornwall, a gorgeous trip which led to me writing a list of similar pub paddle day trips in *The Guardian*, where I was the travel editor (later I freelanced then moved to *The Times* and *Sunday Times*).

As a northerner with family in the north east, living in London but travelling around the UK constantly for work, I've tried to cover a good geographical spread of routes, though inevitably there are perhaps a few more in the most popular holiday regions such as the south west and the Lake District – sorry about that. Please let me know where I've missed.

The maps and directions given are a start point for your own paddle. You should also do your own route planning, check weather conditions, tide times if relevant, get local advice and use other tools and apps to check routes and up-to-date information. The excellent Go Paddling website (*gopaddling.info*), of Paddle UK,

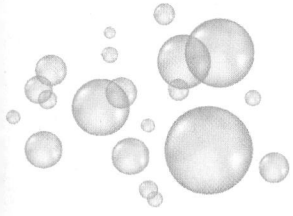

the organisation formerly known as British Canoeing, has great details of most routes, as well as safety advice and articles. You can book your British Waterways licence there too, something you need in order to paddle many of England's, Wales' and Northern Ireland's waterways independently (a right to roam applies to Scottish waters). On guided trips and with hire vessels you won't need one.

Embracing the paddle lifestyle is a lot of fun, and there are so many different ways to approach it, from choosing a little, easy muck-about route of a mile or less, partly as an excuse for hitting the pub after, to longer forays with several stop-offs filling a whole day or more.

To me, paddling is about exploring rather than improving speeds and fitness (though that tends to come for free). It's most akin to hiking in that way: a method for getting to grips with a landscape. Sometimes that means deviating off your route to nose into little gullies or tributaries, to nestle in among the greenery, to leap out onto a bank, or examine sea rocks from all angles. I've seen people embrace paddling in all sorts of ways, from an old guy training hard on his local river to one young dude on a hot summer's day in Hampshire, lying on his SUP alone with his shades on, legs dangling in the green water, sipping a beer and listening to his tunes on his phone, just drifting – the picture of idyllic laziness.

For families a mini paddle adventure can be a great way to bond and to instil hardiness and resilience (all the better with the promise of a lemonade at the end). It can be romantic – take a picnic, therapeutic – take a mate to talk to, or just a useful way to get from A to B – all the better when that 'B' is one of this country's most wonderful waterside pubs.

And as I set off on the Chichester paddle, one of my guides commented that he liked the idea of a pub paddle because it reminded him of the 'chippy hikes' he used to do in Scouts, a long slog of a walk to reach the chip shop for dinner, then a hike back again. There's something about the incentive of a cosy or refreshing stop-off to motivate you on your journey.

The summer I dedicated to paddling to research this book left me fitter, stronger, and, I reckon, looking more relaxed than I had in decades – the zen magic to being on the water, I put that down to. Studies have shown we humans are more relaxed when our gaze

falls frequently to the distance, and indeed when we are near water. Paddling provides both.

Sometimes, after paddling for hours, I wondered if I'd fallen asleep. I'd been in such a state of semi-stupor, not thinking, just being and observing, definitely not stressing. Liquid meditation.

Sometimes, being waterborne makes you feel celebratory. I've felt the urge to yell 'happy birthday!' to a passing boat fluttering with '60 today' helium balloons, to grin and wave at every passing paddler, to shout out to rowers swishing by too arrogantly fast in Cambridge: 'you need a bell mate!' – not something I would do on foot. But being on the water loosens you up: you feel different, joyful, a bit silly.

I got to like paddling in all weathers, in icy Scotland in December, and in pouring rain, when big fat droplets fell all around, making ripple art of an empty river, like neolithic cup and ring stone markings. Even when the water was brown, in the Tees and the Severn, it looked beautiful, like toffee or gravy, rich and peaty. Other times, in the sea near St Agnes, Cornwall, it was so clear I could see rocks forming underwater rooms many metres below.

Canals, lagoons, wild wind-whipped lakes, all have their pleasures - and, thankfully, their pubs too.

TOP: Wherever people want to go, someone will have opened a pub – whether alongside a river or canal, beside a lake or loch, or right on the coast.

Through paddling I've discovered many great spots: inns that boaters have warmed themselves in for centuries, some predating the bridges that cross the rivers, others with their own unique quirks, like the brewery in Hampshire that lowers your pint down to you on your paddleboard.

I also discovered a whole new world of water-folk. Those whose back gardens descend onto rivers have a clandestine, privileged lifestyle I never knew existed, where they lie reading in hammocks by the water and a little hand-built jetty, with canoes pulled up on their lawn, ready to set out on a whim. Plenty of people, it turns out, spend their weekends slumbering in rowing boats full of plump pillows, a bottle of champagne tucked in, clinking glasses and motoring to pubs. But paddling has more of a taste of freedom I reckon. The silence and ease with which you can cut through the water, seeing wildlife at eye level, sitting right in the depths, is unbeatable. Especially when there's a pint waiting at the end.

Water quality

I wrote this book at a time of huge significance for the rivers and waterways, seas and lakes of Britain. Almost all are currently disastrously polluted, and pressure groups and campaigners from grassroots level to the House of Commons fight for action. When even our beloved Lake District lake, Windermere, has raw sewage pumped into it on a regular basis, and the Wye has become something of an open gutter thanks to runoff from local chicken farms, livestock manure, and sewage being released illegally, destroying their ecosystems, the picture looks bleak.

In 2023 Natural England downgraded the river Wye's status to 'unfavourable – declining'. But that's not to denigrate the natural beauty there – to a visitor, our waterways' poor states are not always apparent to the naked eye of the paddler. It was only on very rare occasion that I saw toilet paper piled on the banks, or suspicious foams on the surface. A couple of times I took dips that resulted in rashes (the Thames), showing the importance of rinsing your kit after each paddle, and not letting the water in your mouth.

Yet it surprised me how clear and beautiful, and full of life, most waterways seem to be. Up and down the country they are teeming with wonderful species – beavers and otters are returning, banks are often a jungle of bulrushes, buzzed by kingfishers and soundtracked by toads and the calls of all manner of birds. It is a glorious universe to silently slip into, among the melee, observing and becoming part of it.

The unforgivable pollution should be a drive to celebrate and protect our waterways, and to advocate for them. Avoiding them will only play into the hands of those at fault. Life there is holding on, just, and using them is one of the best things we can do. Campaign if you can, vote for their preservation, but show the world we appreciate and need them, too. It is much easier for the government to ignore the pollution of forgotten waterways that no one seems to care about than well-used places of leisure, where children splash and elders swim, where triathlons and surf competitions take place, and where we paddlers paddle.

Safety

As a paddler, you should already be familiar with general safety advice, so please familiarise yourself with more detailed information on the subject before setting out. Paddle UK's Paddle-Safe Campaign, and joint guidelines from the Royal National Lifeboat Institute (RNLI), Paddle UK, HM Coastguard and paddle companies and retailers is a great resource, whose most important points are to always, always wear a buoyancy aid, tell someone where you're going, carry a mobile phone, check the weather and know your limits. Every type of water has its dangers.

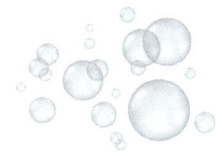

BELOW: This book toasts the best of British pubs, and paddling to or from the rural ones is a great way to explore the countryside (photo: iStock).

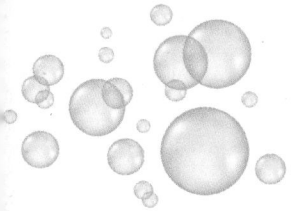

If paddling in the sea, do not go out when there is offshore wind (which can blow you away from shore), check conditions and seek local advice, do not go out if you are not absolutely certain you are capable. Rivers can also take you by surprise. Their condition can vary hugely, especially following rainfall when they are higher and more powerful. Paddleboarders should know to always use a waist leash and not one around the ankle when paddling in moving water – this is an extremely important piece of advice that sadly many people seem unaware of, but it is crucial to being able to release yourself if you become stuck, and an error which has led to numerous fatalities. See *gopaddling.info/blog/tips-and-advice/safe-paddle-summer* and the leading SUP brand Red Paddle's tips, which also highlights checking your equipment carefully before setting out, that you are appropriately dressed, and are fully aware of the weather forecast *red-equipment.co.uk/pages/sup-safety-stay-safe-on-the-water*.

Practicalities

Useful apps and websites include *riverlevels.uk* and *check-for-flooding.service.gov.uk*; the My Tide Times app for checking the tides for coastal paddles and tidal estuaries, and Windy. Strava and Go Paddling apps have route plotting, and look out for Wild Otter App, which my kayak guide in Shrewsbury, Kieran Johnson is developing, with detailed information on paddle routes.

Equipment

I have to thank the SUP market leader Red Paddle (*red-equipment.co.uk*) for lending me a splendid all-round paddleboard for researching this book, and Decathlon (*decathlon.co.uk/sports/kayaking/inflatable-kayaks*) for a very decent inflatable Itiwit kayak, which did my family proud on many an expedition (and can't be blamed for the loss of a child's treasured fishing net that was lost overboard near Salcombe).

> 'Voyager upon life's sea,
> To yourself be true,
> And whatever your lot may be,
> Paddle your own canoe.'
>
> From *Paddle Your Own Canoe* (Sarah T. Bolton)

The Southwest

Cornwall

1 St Agnes Heritage Coastline and The Driftwood Spars

- 4km (2.5 miles)
- Coastal, dramatic, caves
- Sea
- Out and back
- No licence needed

A cave system and rock formations comparable to those you might find in Thailand make this north Cornish coastal paddle a phenomenally beautiful one.

The St Agnes Heritage Coastline offers one of the most visually striking paddles in the country, taking in cliffs streaked with copper, oxidised into vivid shades of turquoise and blue, as if someone tipped several barrels of bright paint down the rocks. There are caves so mind-blowing you won't believe you're in England. It's somewhere that should be as famous as the Giant's Causeway, or the rock stacks of the Scottish islands, yet it's something of a secret, generally only seen by sea kayakers.

Koru Kayaking runs superb guided trips along this part of the north coast of Cornwall (as well as on the Helford River), and in May I took one and set out between low craggy rocks ('rock gardens', our guide Tom Wildblood called them) from St Agnes's

BELOW: Oxidised copper in the rocks near St Agnes on a Koru Kayaking tour.

THE SOUTHWEST

beach, Trevaunance Cove, ten miles south-west of Newquay. Soon we encountered seals, great big bruisers who floated upright like bristle-whiskered buoys. 'They sleep like that,' explained Tom. In November seals breed in coves at the end of rocky corridors here and you can't go near, but in summer, when sunshine burns off the sediment in the water so it's glass-clear and lit by bright light, you can see their silver forms flash by beneath your paddle.

All along the cliff faces heading north are the remnants of mine workings from the once thriving Cornish tin industry. According to Tom, this tin was considered the best in the world in the 1820s, and used for all sorts of products globally. Some of the deep gullies we paddled through were partly natural, partly blasted out by miners' dynamite. We kayaked through a deep double archway called Gadger that felt like a fairground ride.

Granite and other complex rocks mix to dazzling effect where oxidation has worked artistic magic on sections of the cliffs, forming a natural gallery that only the waterborne could enjoy. Some resemble abstract paintings or Aboriginal rock art, with splatter stripes of bright green-blue streaked against ochre and burnt orange as if slathered there by a talented hand.

Then came the black gaping maw of a cave tunnel. Tom and another guide, Ize Neal, steered us through as we paddled cautiously into the cave-mouth, dragging the kayaks up onto the rocks within and clambering through the dripping darkness, avoiding seaweedy pools, until we came to a small light opening at the other end. Then we were expelled into a huge roofless cathedral, the Prison, a chill and damp fallen cave whose soaring walls glistened with tangerine and neon green. Eat your heart out, Koh Phangan.

As to the pub? Two hours after starting out we were back at the

CLOCKWISE FROM TOP RIGHT: Atlantic grey seals can be spotted; paddling through natural arches; the Prison fallen cavern; Gemma and son on the tour; crystal clear waters near St Agnes.

beach and walked up the steep hill, bypassing **Schooners**, another decent drinking spot overlooking the beach, for locals' favourite **The Driftwood Spars**. Here plumbers, millionaires, fishermen and celebs mix in together and chew the fat over local Sea Shanty ales; one table is always reserved for the regulars – AKA the Four O'Clock Club. (Tom explains it used to be called the Five O'Clock Club until they decided to start boozing earlier.) Snug, characterful and with its own microbrewery, it's an awesome spot.

▶ Details
Koru Kayaking (*korukayaking.co.uk*) runs tours from St Agnes. Be warned they can be adversely affected by weather conditions and may be rerouted, sometimes heading south instead. Independent paddlers can launch from the beach. See (*visitstagnes.com*). For the pubs, see (*verdantbrewing.co/pages/schooners-st-agnes-verdant*) and (*driftwoodspars.co.uk*).

▶ Make a weekend of it
The Driftwood Spars has seaview rooms, or for a brilliant way to see this coastline, hire the Scarangar bus (*scarangar.com*), which sleeps ten in bunks and comes with a guide and driver, who cooks for you (there's a kitchen onboard and a lounge) and drives you to different campsites, local pubs and attractions.

ABOVE: Sheer rockfaces add plenty of drama to this route.

LEFT: The Driftwood Spars.

Cornwall

2 River Helford and the Ferry Boat Inn

- 5.1km (3.2 miles)
- Coastal, holiday vibes, nature
- Tidal river
- Out and back
- No licence needed

Cornwall's captivating southern limb, the Lizard peninsula, has the bone-white sands, iridescent peacock-coloured water and sculptural rock formations summer holiday dreams are made of. Epic sea paddles are a great way to take all this in. But for the casual paddler not wanting to take on the Atlantic waves, the area also offers otherworldly gullies lagoon-like channels banked by tree-topped cliffs, palms and Monterey pines. Exploring them by SUP or kayak can feel like exploring the Amazon... except there's often a characterful pub at the end.

The most atmospheric perhaps is the River Helford, Britain's most southerly river, whose tributaries include Frenchman's Creek, famously the inspiration for the eponymous book by Daphne du Maurier, who honeymooned there. There are so many creeks that the Helford's shoreline is five times longer than the river's length. Flowing out on the western side of the peninsula south of Falmouth, the river – a ria, or inundated river valley – passes through two villages, Helford Passage on the north, Helford on the south, with a (very short) ferry linking the two. There has been a

BELOW: The pretty village of Helford.

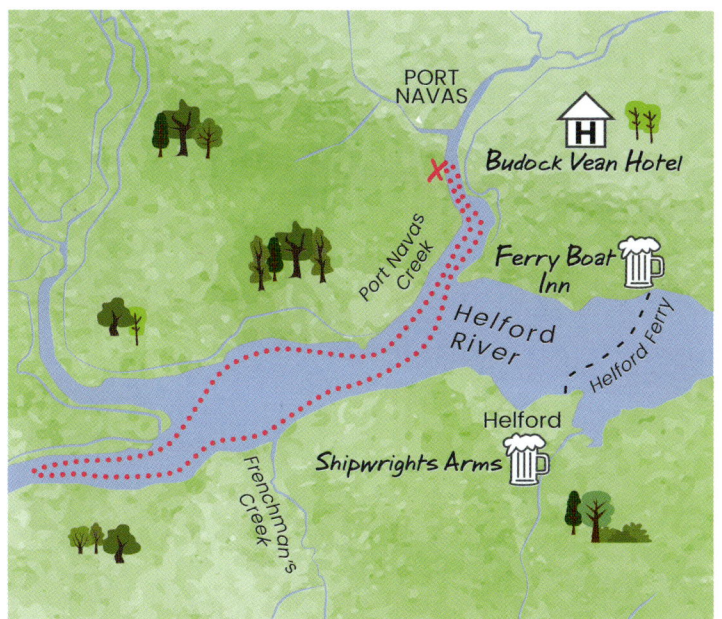

ferry boat here for 1,000 years, and records of the named ferrymen date back to 1283.

Each of the pretty villages has a car park and a good pub in front of which you can launch.

Why not paddle a route between them, zigzagging from one side to the other, up and down the tidal river when the water's high enough.

The Ferry Boat Inn in Helford Passage has outdoor seating overlooking the small beach, where some take a pint to sit on the beach wall. People often launch SUPs and inflatable kayaks for a mess-around paddle in the evenings here. Inside, old photos of fisherfolk cover the walls, and mackerel tacos and schnitzel are signature dishes.

On the other side, the wonderfully characterful **Shipwrights Arms** lies at the end of the delightful enclave of Helford, which spreads along the estuary, and where pretty white cottages line the steep roads down to the water, their walls overflowing with pink and white daisies. The pub's staggered decks sit above the water, a mermaid figurehead surveying the scene. Eat bowls of scampi and squid with a glass of Tribute or Pimms, looking out over seaweedy lobster pots, kids crabbing, and seagulls hovering above. Heaven.

BELOW: This way to the pub.

FROM TOP: Gemma and family on the Helford River tour; the beach outside the Ferry Boat Inn; paddling past the Powders shipwreck on the Helford, and sign for another local cafe; the Shipwrights Arms.

LEFT: The banks of the Helford River are home to ancient oak woodlands.

BELOW: Koru Kayaking runs tours of the Helford.

To go between the two pubs, you can choose to paddle, take a ferry ride (check the times), or a 40-minute drive in a big loop around the estuary, down lanes deep in ferns.

One of the UK's best kayak and SUP operators – Koru Kayaking – has a base at the bottom of the gardens of the Budock Vean Hotel, on the north side of the Helford on Port Navas creek. (Please check as there was a chance the base might move after the publication of this book).

You'll feel like you're walking into the pages of a novel when you arrive, descending past the hotel's trim lawns through a corridor of giant gunneras, tree ferns and pink rhododendrons to Koru's beachside cafe and base.

Koru's co-owners, Hetty and Tom Wildblood (whose names surely belong in an adventure novel) chucked in their corporate careers with plans to move to New Zealand. But when they happened upon the Lizard, they realised the climactic landscapes and natural raw beauty they were dreaming of existed right here, so they pivoted their plans to create one of Cornwall's first paddle businesses instead.

Tom led us on a three mile tour of the river around high tide, when Frenchman's Creek, upstream, is accessible. Other tours go downriver to Grebe beach.

Using Wilderness Systems kayaks – 'the heavier the better with kayaks,' said Tom, 'as the wind is your enemy' – we crossed a channel that is in part 30m (100ft) deep, below hills studded with cloud-scraping Monterey pines. These were the fashionable thing to plant 150 years ago, though their weak roots means they are liable to tumble down any time now.

Heading towards Frenchman's Creek, we passed Powders, a 1930s National Trust wooden bungalow owned by an artist and sailor who went by that name, perhaps because he kept a shotgun and didn't like people coming near; you can see his 150-year old boat, eroding on the shore. Osprey and kingfishers may appear, and bass, wrasse and mullet dwell in these waters; certainly something large often sploshed near our paddles.

We passed a load of young people hanging out on a fallen tree protruding from the water. 'Do you know the significance of the tree you're standing on?' yelled Tom. 'No idea!' they replied. I expected him to reveal some nugget of natural history, or a tawdry tale about the river's smuggling history but no, he informed us: 'Kylie Minogue shot a video on it!'

On the return leg we stopped at one of many little coves to swim in cool silky jade water, then glided back under oaks twisted by the sea. 'We don't have caves on this side of Cornwall,' said Tom, 'but we do have tree caves.'

Back on land we sat for a while on the soft grassy banks with a can of local Beacon pale ale from Koru's cafe, dusting sand from our toes, before setting off for the pub.

OPPOSITE: Views of the river from the Ferry Boat Inn.

▶ Details

Book a tour with Koru Kayaks (*korukayaking.co.uk*); or hire kayaks and SUPS from Helford River Boats (*helfordriverboats.co.uk*). For the ferry, see (*helfordriverboats.co.uk/the-ferry*). For pubs, see (*ferryboatcornwall.co.uk*) and (*shipwrights-helford.co.uk*). The National Trust has a launch at Durgan for a fee (*nationaltrust.org.uk/visit/cornwall/bosveal/sailing-and-kayaking-on-the-helford-river*).

▶ Make a weekend of it

The National Trust's Powders (*nationaltrust.org.uk/holidays/cornwall/powders*) sleeps four on the creek edge, or in Helford, Kestle Barton (*kestlebarton.co.uk*) is a gorgeous collection of cottages of various sizes around an art gallery and beautiful garden.

Cornwall

3 The Fal Estuary to the Pandora Inn

- 4.8km (3 miles)
- Fun, lively, interesting
- Tidal estuary
- Out and back
- No licence needed

There can't be many British sailors who haven't heard of the **Pandora Inn**. Ask anyone about the best and most famous Cornish pubs and its name is sure to come up. This delightful waterside spot is legendary among yachties and motor-boaters who putter over to tie up at its long pontoon for a glass of wine over the shimmering water. Cyclists and hikers stop by too, admiring its thatched roof and pretty blue window-frames, and many drivers know it as an easy stop-off en route down the A39 along the south Cornish coast. You will find it tucked away on Restronguet Creek, one of the tributaries of Carrick Roads (the estuary of the River Fal that runs out by Falmouth).

You and I know, of course, that the best way to arrive is by paddling, as sunshine turns the water to scattered diamonds. You can pull in on the tiny crescent of sand for a swift St Austell Ale, or a long lazy lunch of whitebait and Pandora fish pie, all very fresh and reliant on local, seasonal produce.

There is no record of what the inn was first known as, back in the 13th century when it was probably a farm cottage. Later it became the Passage House, where a boat was kept to cross the water and speed the way for travellers between Falmouth and Truro. Then it was known as The Ship, but became the Pandora in

BELOW: The Pandora Inn from the water.

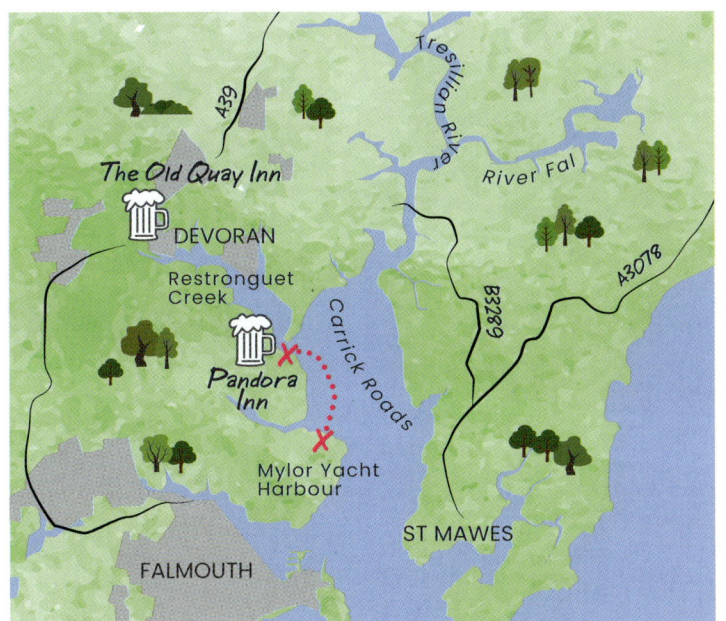

memory of a naval vessel that was sent to Tahiti to capture mutineers from the Bounty in 1790. The frigate struck part of the Great Barrier Reef and sank, many men were lost, and its captain – Edwards – returned to Britain to be court martialled, then exonerated. It is rumoured – by the pub for one – that he bought and ran the venue in his retirement, though there's no hard evidence of the fact.

Nevertheless, the name stuck.

You could take weeks exploring every nook and hidden cove of the estuary and river, but a good place to start out from is Mylor Yacht Harbour, on the west side of Falmouth, especially if you need hire or a guide. From here it's a 40-minute paddle at a fairly slow pace. I did it with my nine-year-old daughter on a tour starting from Falmouth River Watersports, she on a SUP, me on a kayak (then me inevitably towing her SUP behind me when she got bored). How could you be bored really though, with so much to see, from rolling hillsides to a party boat pumping out music with guests dancing on the roof. Falmouth's sailing community is thriving and varied, providing plenty of entertainment.

During the colder months of the year, you might see dolphins, and seals, too, down by the King Harry Ferry up the River Fal, as well as egrets, grebes and kingfishers at the quieter end of the

BELOW: The paddle to the pub from Mylor is about 40 minutes.

CLOCKWISE FROM TOP LEFT: The characterful Pandora Inn's interior; the coastal village of St Mawes; the Fal estuary from St Mawes; a furry passenger.

ABOVE: Trelissick House on the River Fal (photo: iStock).

day. A three hour rental or tour gives plenty of time to get to the pub and back, but there are beaches and swimming spots to spend time on if you have it.

▶ Details

Falmouth River Watersports (*falmouthriverwatersports.co.uk*) offers hire of kayaks and SUPs from Mylor Yacht Harbour, and excellent tours, including one using an electric boat in one direction. It also has a sailing school. See (*pandorainn.com*).

▶ Make a weekend of it

In Falmouth, the hip Star and Garter (*starandgarterfalmouth.co.uk*) is a Georgian townhouse pub with super interior design in its harbour view rooms and apartments, and posh food such as ricotta dumplings and crispy monkfish. Across the water in St Mawes, the Rising Sun (*risingsunstmawes.co.uk*) is a cool, revamped St Austell brewery pub above the beach. Or try Creekside Cottages (*creeksidecottages.co.uk*) and Helpful Holidays (*helpfulholidays.co.uk*) for self-catering.

▶ Alternative routes

Further into Restronguet Creek, **The Old Quay Inn** (*theoldquayinn.co.uk*) in Devoran feels hidden away, with a riverside beer garden. Higher up the estuary, where the River Fal converges with the Truro and Tresilian rivers, the **Heron Inn** (*heroninnmalpas.co.uk*) in Malpas welcomes paddlers with beautiful green views. It's a four-hour trip from Mylor or quicker if you go half way in an electric boat on a tour with Falmouth River Watersports.

3 THE FAL ESTUARY

Cornwall

4 River Fowey: Golant to Lerryn

- 6.4km (4 miles)
- Gentle, natural, fun
- Tidal river
- Out and back
- Licence needed

Sailing boats festoon the harbour of the chic and arty fishing village of Fowey, once Cornwall's most important medieval port, at a time when fish, tin and wool were traded with Europe, and pirates ruled the roost. Sirs Francis Drake and Walter Raleigh sailed from here, and it is where Henry VIII erected St Catherine's Castle to protect against the French.

Now though, it's the smart small-plate restaurants and micro galleries that will relieve you of your money, rather than mischievous old salts. Chic outlets are squeezed in among the fish and chip shops and characterful old pubs, while millionaire mansions line the shores around the town.

Hire in Fowey, or take your own kayak or SUP to launch from busy Fowey Harbour (fees apply), paddling among the seagulls, fishing boats and posh yachts.

Upstream, all is peaceful – the upper River Fowey is a place to dally and drift, with hidden nooks, coves and secret channels to explore. It's a tranquil world of blurry blue-green water.

A good place to set out is Golant, a village on the west bank two miles north of Fowey, with a car park and public access to the water.

Guided tours are available here with Encounter Cornwall. They start from the small quay where the company has its base, the Boatshed, and where it also hires out SUPS and kayaks, alongside a small cafe for all your pasty and proper coffee needs. Practically next door is the **Fisherman's Arms** with a waterside beer garden – so head there after your trip.

A different pub was the objective of this tour, though – **The Ship Inn** in Lerryn, an enclave on the eastern tributary, the River Lerryn. This trip is easily replicated by anyone with their own kit,

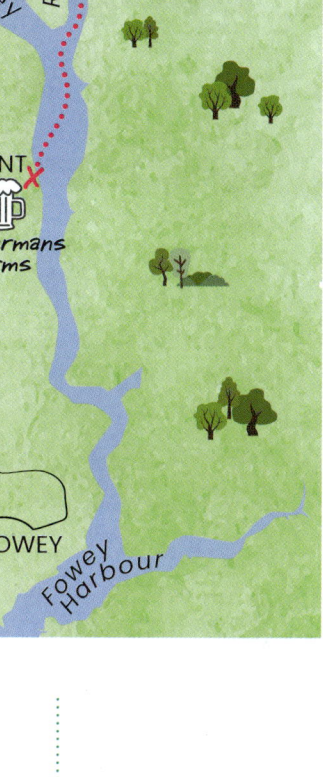

OPPOSITE: Fowey on a summer's day.

LEFT: The River Fowey from above.

4 RIVER FOWEY 29

CLOCKWISE FROM TOP LEFT: The Ship Inn; Fowey harbour; Pont Pil on the Fowey estuary; setting out from Golant.

THE SOUTHWEST

but the three-hour 'Creeks and Backwaters' relaxed group tour was a chance to learn about local wildlife and history, paddling with the tides, passing prettily coloured cottages and quiet coves. In Lerryn we pulled up on the shore and crossed the road to the Ship, a sweet and characterful pub, taken over by a new team in 2023 that offers community-minded camaraderie and live music.

▶ Details

Encounter Cornwall (*encountercornwall.com*) – also known as Paddle Cornwall SUP – offers this pub paddle trip, as well as kayak and SUP hire, which can be extended by a few days for the duration of a holiday. For the pubs, see (*fishermansarmsgolant.co.uk*) and (*theshipinnlerryn.co.uk*). Users of the Fowey River have been required since 2022 to register with Fowey Harbour as a matter of safety, and should purchase a licence (*foweyharbour.co.uk/stay-safe-register-your-sups-and-kayaks*).

▶ Make a weekend of it

The kayaking former owners of Paddle Cornwall have launched accommodation overlooking the Fowey Estuary in the form of The Sanctuary Cornwall (*thesanctuarycornwall.co.uk*), with B&B rooms, a self-catering apartment and cabin, and the Ship Inn has a few colourfully painted bedrooms.

BELOW: A kayak tour with Encounter Cornwall.

Devon

5 Bigbury-on-Sea to Burgh Island

- 0.8km (½ mile)
- Coastal, historic, beach
- Sea
- Circular
- No licence needed

The **Pilchard Inn**, on Burgh Island, reckons it has been 'quenching the island's thirst since 1336'. This tiny islet is connected by a natural tidal causeway to the sweeping sandy beach of Bigbury-on-Sea on the south Devon coast. Back in that far distant year, it was the island's fishermen that supped in the cosy confines of its flagstoned parlours. Later, smugglers and wreckers connived in its darkened nooks. On my last trip, I recognised newspaper columnists and media darlings there – perhaps just as conniving as their predecessors, but dealing in a more subtle form of loot.

The island's famous and fabulous place to stay, the **Burgh Island Hotel**, has long been booked out by vintage lovers, who

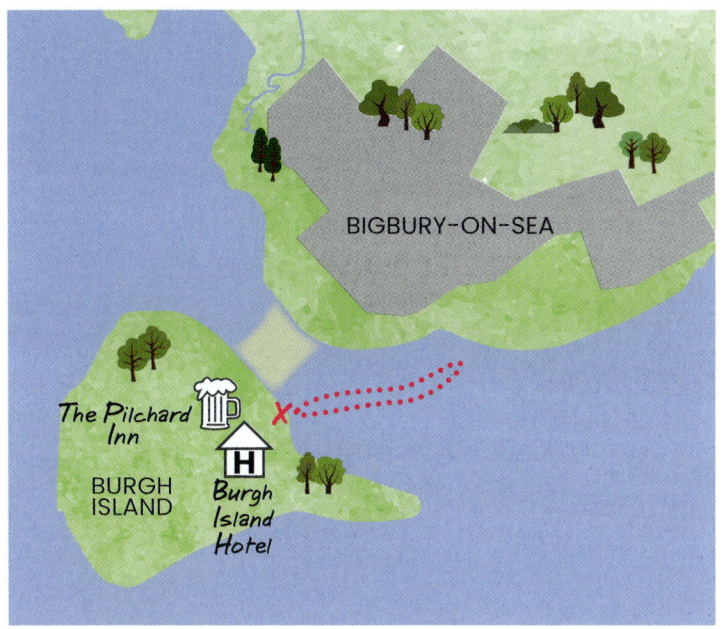

come for the Art Deco stylings of this 1920s/30s marvel, usually in era-appropriate gladrags to a soundtrack of live jazz. This unique hotel, with its fine dining and ballroom, may be the most famous spot on the rock, but the island pub is just as beguiling, with stone-flagged floors and wooden beams, and low ceilings perfect for a smugglers' purlieu.

At low tide it's possible to walk over to the island from Bigbury-on-Sea's beach along the natural sandbar, but once there's a bit of depth most visitors climb aboard the sturdy old sea tractor. This unique hydraulic passenger vehicle is the only one of its kind, with an open carriage above huge wheels that allow it to chug through water. It was designed in the late 1960s by Robert Jackson, an engineer involved in the development of UK nuclear power stations in the 1950s. Appropriately for this frolicsome island, he was paid for the design of the sea tractor with a case of champagne.

As tempting as the sea tractor might be, you and I know that it's even more fun to paddle across. With your own kit you can park at Bigbury-on-Sea car park a short distance away. Be mindful of the vagaries of the current, which can be strong and occasionally a little bit funky around the island. You can paddle all the way around in about an hour to explore the crannies and

OPPOSITE: Burgh Island from the mainland (photo: Burgh Island).

CLOCKWISE FROM TOP LEFT: Inside the pub; benches overlook the sea; you can walk across to the Pilchard Inn at low tide.

THE SOUTHWEST

smugglers' caves around the back, but heed local advice. The pub's outdoor terrace overlooks the water so you can survey the tide while enjoying your icy drink and fish and chips. For a longer paddle, take in Hope Cove to the south, a protected harbour that's good for beginners, passing the popular surf beach of Bantham – but only link them all if conditions are good and you're experienced.

LEFT: Burgh Island's swimming spot, the Mermaid Pool (photo: Burgh Island).

❯ Details
Hire paddle or surfboards and kayaks on Bigbury's beach from Discovery Surf (*discoverysurf.com*). For more information, see Visit Devon's webpage (*visitsouthdevon.co.uk/things-to-do/bigbury-on-sea-beach*) and Burgh Island's (*burghisland.com*).

❯ Make a weekend of it
The Burgh Island Hotel (*burghisland.com/hotel*) has a wide variety of luxurious period rooms and cottages. Helpful Holidays (*helpfulholidays.co.uk*) has quite a few seaview cottages in the Bigbury area.

Devon

6 Salcombe Estuary: Kingsbridge to the Millbrook Inn

- 12km (7.5 miles)
- Coastal, foodie, beaches
- Estuary
- One way
- No licence needed

Devon's wonderful estuaries are one of its defining and perhaps most winning features. The Rivers Exe and Dart, and the Salcombe Estuary crack the landscape with their captivating gullies and narrow tributaries then come tumbling out into wider river mouths with harbours, pretty coves and long sandy beaches that were seemingly made for the waterborne. Hidden among them are many fantastic pubs, once riddled with smugglers, now drawing the country's foodies. You could fill weeks exploring them all, but I've picked a few of the best to start with.

The Kingsbridge-Salcombe estuary is unusual in that it has no major river feeding it, but has creeks, beaches and fishing villages along its shores, many hiding secretive, timeless pubs. As it is strongly tidal, the furthest, tightest reaches are only accessible at high tide, so you'll have to take your pick of which bits to explore in a day, or risk being stranded by trying to do too much. Ideally, get someone to collect you at the end of a one-way trip, or do a two-car shuffle so you don't have to do the return of this suggested journey.

BELOW: North Sands beach, near Salcombe.

Start out from Kingsbridge, where there's a car park right by the slipway, and a glossy pub, **The Crabshell Inn**, on the waterside. One of many in the south-west operated by the St Austell brewery group, this smart option has octopus tentacle artwork slinking across the ceiling and good pizzas, fish and chips and seafood sharing plates and a waterside terrace. Decent for lunch before setting off, or a post-paddle party. Try to set off with the outgoing tide, so you're not going against the current (it can be windy here too, and you don't want a double battle on your hands).

Enjoy the views of the South Hams' elephantine hills as you paddle hard into this wide open waterway. You'll find that when the narrower Kingsbridge Estuary joins the main thrust of the Salcombe Estuary you're among a lot more river users –

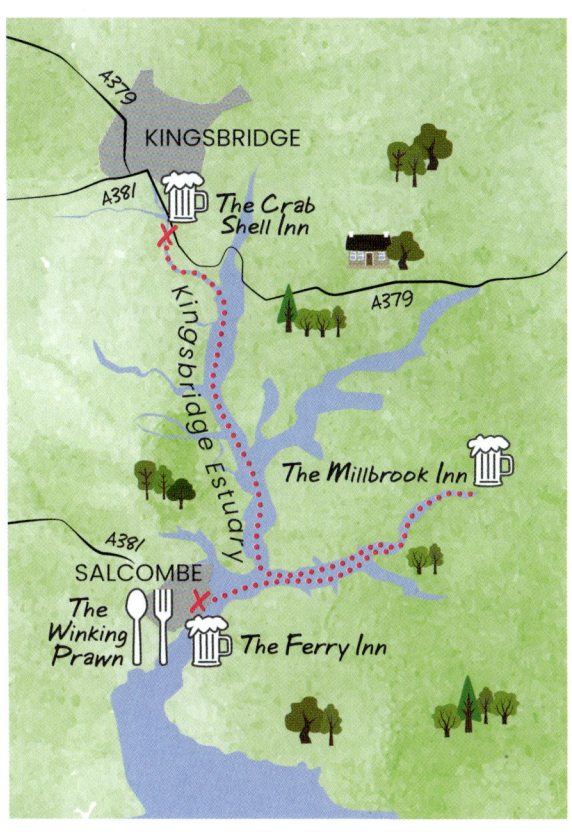

dinghies, motorboats, other paddlers, sail boats. Stick close to shore where beaches are laced with seaweed and defined by barnacle-covered rocks.

Just as you see Salcombe on the right-hand, western shore, take the tidal creek opposite and paddle hard to make it upstream to the tiny village of South Pool. You can't quite paddle right up to the pub but the river dwindles to a stream and gets you close. **The Millbrook Inn** is one of the most originally and creatively styled pubs in the southwest, with a truly excellent restaurant to match. Local fare from the owner family's Fowlescombe Farm and fish from day boats are whipped into plates such as ox tongue carpaccio with crispy capers, Dartmouth crab and lobster cocktail or Salcombe lobster with wild garlic. It's served in low-ceilinged, firelit flagstone rooms with racing green panelling and vintage lights. Make it here for lunch or dinner (book ahead; the website handily supplies high tide times to help you get there) and you'll be treated to one of the finest feasts in the county. This side of the

BELOW: Outside the Crabshell Inn.

CLOCKWISE FROM TOP LEFT: The Ferry Inn, Salcombe; a view over the estuary; the Crabshell Inn's terrace near Kingsbridge; Salcombe's North Sands beach.

estuary has Caribbean-looking beaches to spend time on and, if you're crossing back over the estuary to Salcombe, it'd be rude not to pop into **The Ferry Inn**, one of many historic pubs in this chichi harbour town. Even if you have come all this way via both pubs (12km/7.5 mile of paddling so far), you might want to add on the **Winking Prawn** beach cafe around the corner, a fun and funky spot with good fishy snacks.

▶ Details

Find information on the route at the tourist board website (*visitsouthdevon.co.uk/explore/south-devon-map*). For the pubs, see (*thecrabshellinn.co.uk*), (*millbrookinnsouthpool.co.uk*), (*theferryinnsalcombe.com*) and (*winkingprawn.co.uk*). For SUP lessons and hire from Kingsbridge try Waterborne (*waterborn.uk.com*), which also runs 'paddle and pick' tours to collect plastic floating in the water. Hire paddleboards and get lessons from Kingsbridge from Sup Walk (*supwalk.com*); or from Dartmouth along the coast, with Sea Kayak Devon (*seakayakdevon.co.uk*), which also runs wild camping kayak trips.

▶ Make a weekend of it

The Millbrook Inn (*millbrookinnsouthpool.co.uk*) has two gorgeous adjoining cottages, each with two rooms, so sleeping four.

BELOW: The Winking Prawn.

Devon

7 River Dart: Stoke Gabriel to the Maltsters Arms, Tuckenhay

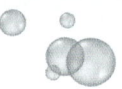

- 10.5km (6.5 miles)
- Fun, coastal, exploration
- Tidal estuary/river
- Out and back
- No licence needed

One of the UK's original and most flamboyant telly chefs, Keith Floyd, who beguiled the nation in the 1980s with his irreverent, wine-fuelled cook ups filmed en plein air, owned the 18th-century **Maltsters Arms** in Tuckenhay between 1989 and 1996. He spent millions doing it up, adding eccentrically-decorated bedrooms and anchoring fake crocodiles in the water outside, reportedly to scare the tourists.

Now, somewhat less wacky, but still with a 'Keith Floyd' private dining room, the pub makes an excellent port of call on a paddle along the River Dart from Stoke Gabriel, a sweet village four miles south from the quirky town of Totnes. The Maltsers lies down the first channel west after heading downriver from Stoke Gabriel, on Bow Creek, a tributary that can dry out at low tide. It's crucial to come during the five hours across high tide when it's accessible to a metre's depth, with a pontoon that rises and falls.

There are so many different ways to approach exploring this beautiful river and estuary, and many great pubs hidden among its veins. Totnes, infamous liberal hippy hotpot of alternative living,

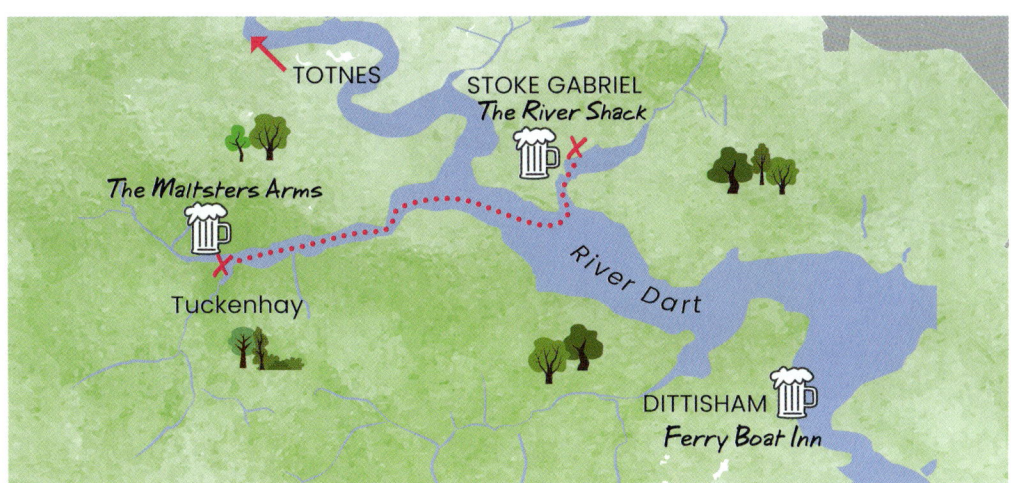

is an interesting town to meander around – with many health food stores, hip cafes such as The Hairy Barista, with nutty green smoothies, plaster-pink walls and macrame hangings, shops selling crystals or Danish fashion, and the cool **Bull Inn**, a chic 'organic, ethical' pub with an on-trend 'millennial pink' facade.

Several paddle companies run trips downriver from the town, while independent paddlers can access the water near the Longmarsh or Steamer Quay car parks. At the southern end of Totnes, the **Waterside Bistro** has steps up from the water and rings to tie onto, then a little further south there's the **Steam Packet** Inn. The river is tidal from here so check times to go with the flow.

It's 8km (5 miles) from Totnes to Stoke Gabriel, where smart homes tumble down a steep road to the quayside, a spot for children to go crabbing from beside the weir. The adjoining Mill Pool is a flat and sheltered spot to practise paddling (stay away from the weir) but Stoke Gabriel is a good starting point too for exploring the tidal Dart.

Before you go, or after you get back, **The River Shack** is right by the water and a fun, rustic semi-outdoor venue doing great grilled mackerel, woodfired pizzas, breakfast brioches, local gins, beers and ciders, champagne and wine. Another pub up the hill, the **Church House Inn**, is more traditional.

In addition to visiting Tuckenhay, it's fun to paddle south to the pretty fishing village of Dittisham, where the bright pink **Ferry Boat Inn** is an old fishermen's pub, now reeling in the tourists, with a long pontoon for dinghies coming from Dartmouth and beyond.

OPPOSITE: The River Shack in Stoke Gabriel.

BELOW: Sunset on the Mill Pool at Stoke Gabriel.

7 RIVER DART 41

CLOCKWISE FROM TOP LEFT: Kayaking on the River Dart near Salcombe; the Waterside Bistro, south of Totnes; the Church House Inn, Stoke Gabriel; the Maltsters Arms.

THE SOUTHWEST

You could carry on as far as Dartmouth – 8km (5 miles) from Stoke Gabriel, to the sea, and south to Blackpool Sands.

When I did this route, a seal followed me most of the way back, basking nearby then swimming up behind me, suddenly popping up to surprise me right beside my board.

The famous British paddleboard company, Red Paddle, the OG of the sport, has chosen this spot as its base too, which tells you all you need to know.

▶ Details

For the pubs and cafes, see (*the-maltsters.co.uk*), (*bullinntotnes.co.uk*), (*steampacketinn.co.uk*), (*therivershackdevon.co.uk*), (*fbidittisham.co.uk*) and (*thehairybarista.co.uk*). Hire kayaks from Totnes with Paddle Devon (*paddledevon.co.uk/totnes*), which offers guided trips and lessons. Sea Kayak Devon (*seakayakdevon.co.uk*) runs trips around the Dart including two-day wild camping trips. Totnes Kayaks (*totneskayaks.co.uk*) offers canoe, kayak and paddleboard hire from Stoke Gabriel, as well as guided trips.

Canoe Adventures (*canoeadventures.co.uk*) runs big group trips in giant canoes, and 'paddle to the pub' excursions from Stoke Gabriel to the Ferry Boat Inn, stopping on a beach to build a campfire under the stars on the return. Sea Kayak Devon (*seakayakdevon.co.uk*) runs all sorts of trips and tours from Dartmouth. For information, see tourist board website (*visittotnes.co.uk/enjoy-exploring-the-river-dart-in-totnes*), official paddle trail info (*dartharbour.org*) and Paddle UK's page (*gopaddling.info/rivers/river-dart*).

▶ Make a weekend of it

The Bull Inn (*bullinntotnes.co.uk/rooms*) in Totnes has nine fashionable rooms in pale pinks with panelling, and an apartment. The Maltsters Arms (*the-maltsters.co.uk*) has six rooms in an adjoining building.

▶ Alternative routes

There are so many different options on the Dart Estuary and River Dart. From Totnes, you could paddle upriver to the Dartington Estate, and it's possible to join SUP trips from there heading downriver with Dynamic Adventures (*dynamicadventurescic.co.uk/paddleboarding-devon*) who are based on the estate.

7 RIVER DART

Devon

8 Exeter Quay to the Double Locks Pub

- 4.8km (3 miles)
- Easy, city, fun
- Canal
- Out and back
- Licence needed

Exeter, Devon's cathedral city, is home to a hugely popular and easy dash of a pub paddle that even -those who live in the greener wilds of the county will come into town to join.

Exeter's Historic Quayside has undergone a slick revival in recent years, with waterside warehouses transformed into breweries, bars and cafes. It's from here that the Exeter Ship Canal runs east out of the city, soon falling in parallel with the River Exe as they trundle through sunny green countryside towards the sea. Paddle this route and, within a relaxed 40 minutes, you'll reach the **Double Locks**, a corker of a waterside pub. The traditional red-brick hostelry sits between the River Exe, to the east, and the canal, where a long wooden deck of beer tables stretches beside the water.

This simple, gentle route is very beginner-friendly, and easy to do yourself. AS Watersports, a smart shop selling paddle gear, also hires out kayaks and SUPs on the quayside. The store runs a weekly evening outing in summer paddling to the pub and back for its staff, friends and any keen paddlers who might want to join.

The simplest route to the pub and back is along the canal, but

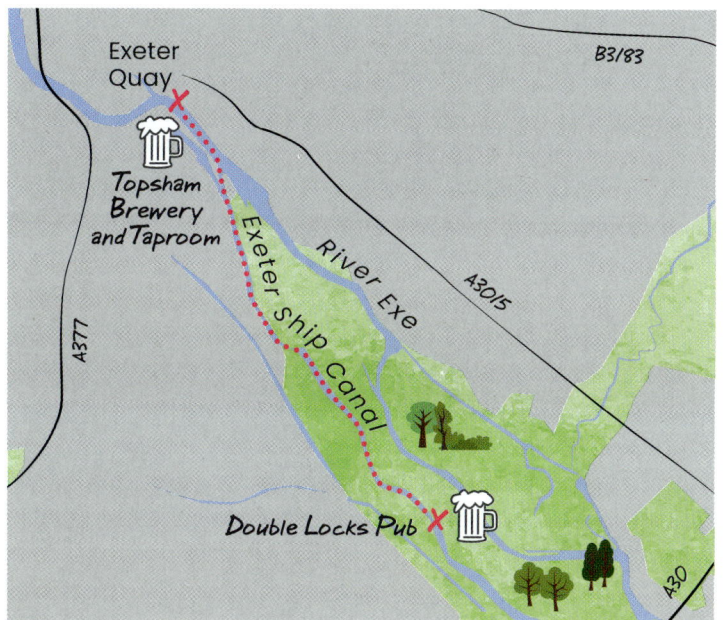

because the River Exe runs almost in parallel, it's possible to portage across to it near the pub – and at other certain points where the two converge – allowing you to make a loop. You will need to go with the tide though, so check times.

Plop into the canal at Exeter Quayside (there's a public car park over the road, next to the Clip 'n' Climb rock climbing centre). If you hire from AS Watersports you can use its pontoon outside the paddle sports centre.

As you head out, you'll pass interesting boats along the banks and on the left, the huge Riverside Country Park, where the city's locals walk, run, cycle and play.

I paddled this route on a joyful summer day, the water a mirror of the cloud-wisped sky. As I approached the pub, a family of swans led the way, and I fell in line behind the cygnets, following them across a flat pool by the locks, where drinkers, walkers, cyclists and paddlers were gathered on the banks. Keeping an eye on their kayaks and SUPs, they clinked pints of local cider and Young's ale in the sun, and ventured around to the tables of the canal-side terrace when it was time to eat. On the river side of the pub, a huge stretch tent covers part of the beer garden for drizzly days. Inside, the pub has a traditional feel yet looks on-the-money cool – perhaps accidentally so – with its forest green ceiling and

OPPOSITE: Exeter's Ship Canal makes for an easy, beginner-friendly paddle.

CLOCKWISE FROM TOP LEFT: The Double Locks pub; the lively Exeter Quayside; the launch from AS Watersports with Topsham Brewery behind; the locks by the pub; swans on the canal.

THE SOUTHWEST

dark wood panelling, its wonky walls hung with natty art and festoon lights. There's a decent menu of classics: ploughman's, sandwiches, and quirkier options such as tempura broccoli, Devon crab salad and a whole list of spritzes for summer. But what people really come for is the vibe: lively without being brash, popular with active types rather than drunkards. The return is quick, and once you're back at the Quayside, pop into the **Topsham Brewery** and tap room, offering juicy IPAs, milkshake stouts and pizzas in a refined industrial setting.

▸ Details

Hire kayaks and paddleboards from AS Watersports (*aswatersports.co.uk*), which also has a map of the Exeter Canoe and Kayak Loops on its website. See the local site (*exeterquay.org*) and Paddle UK's web page (*gopaddling.info/canals/exeter-ship-canal*). For the pubs, see (*doublelocks.com*) and (*topshambrewery.co.uk*).

▸ Make a weekend of it

Exeter has some great places to stay, including the **Turk's Head** micropub and hotel (*turksheadexeter.com*). This dark green drinking den was frequented by Charles Dickens, and now its high ceilings are hung with glam sculptural lighting, while the stylish bedrooms feature raw wood headboards.

▸ Alternative route

After the Double Locks, carry on further south down the canal and you'll come to a swing bridge. Soon after, the river and canal come very close together, enabling a portage so you can create a loop, going back upriver. You'll need to check tide times to go with the flow in both directions on this tidal river. Sometimes vegetation in the water restricts the way, especially at low tide, so get local advice before setting off. Alternatively, stay on the canal and continue all the way to **The Turf** (*the-turf.com*), a Grade II listed, wonky-windowed inn, built in 1827 and recently renovated to add trendy bedrooms. It's next to Turf Lock, which links the river and canal. The next section of the River Exe, from Topsham to Exmouth is challenging with tricky currents, really only for experts, though Exe Adventures (*exeadventures.co.uk*) runs trips, as well as pub paddles to The Turf.

BELOW: Paddleboarding on the canal.

More great paddles in Devon

ABOVE: The banks of the River Exe at Tiverton (photo: iStock).

BELOW: Noss Mayo, home to the Swan Inn (photo: iStock).

NOSS MAYO AND NEWTON FERRERS

On the south coast 16km (10 miles) east of Plymouth, the villages of Newton Ferrers and Noss Mayo lie on either side of Newton Creek, a tributary of the River Yealm, and have a few waterside pubs between them. Top spot, on a little side channel, Noss Creek, is **The Ship Inn** (*theshipinn-nossmayo.co.uk*), which is several centuries old though now has a snazzy terrace overlooking the water. Day boat fish and spritzes are on the menu. Close by is **The Swan Inn** (*swaninnnossmayo.com*), with wooden seating outside, blankets and heaters, and a tight menu of great local fish. Opposite, on the other side of Newton Creek, **The Dolphin** (*dolphininn.weebly.com*) provides a two-tier garden, seafood menus and speciality whiskies. Kayaks come with some of Holiday Cottages Noss Mayo's properties (*holidaycottagesnossmayo.co.uk*).

THE SOUTHWEST

RIVER AXE AND SEATON BAY

In east Devon, the River Axe flows past Axminster and Axmouth and emerges at Seaton Bay, where SB Watersports (*sbwatersports.co.uk*) are the folks for SUP and kayak hire and guided trips. Paddle along the coast to beachy Beer to paddle through sea arches, and to swim at Pounds Pool Beach, only accessible by water. Paddling up the River Axe is another option. It's about 1.6km (1 mile) from Axmouth to the sea, or 14.5km (9 miles) from Axminster. In Axmouth, the family-run **Ship Inn** (*shipinnaxmouth.com*) serves handpicked crabs from Beer, and handpicked beers. Closer to the water, the **Harbour Inn** (*theharbouraxmouth.co.uk*) has a beer garden, a thatched roof and a 12th-century fireplace at its heart.

TIVERTON CANAL

An unusual canalside venue cheers the towpath of the Tiverton Canal, the **Diddy Ducks** floating barge cafe and bar (*tivertoncanal.co.uk/floating-cafe-bar*), which provides artisan coffee, Devon ciders, real ales, draught lager and loose leaf tea

BELOW: The beach at Seaton Bay (photo: iStock).

MORE GREAT PADDLES IN DEVON

to those returning from a spin in the Canadian canoes and rowing boats rented here.

RIVER TEIGN

Wild, grade four rapids provide some fun at its north end, but the Teign's southern reaches, where it becomes an estuary, are peaceful and home to otters and herons. Teignmouth has several pubs, and in nearby Combeinteignhead, the **Coombe Cellars Country Pub** (*thecoombecellars.co.uk*) has a glamorous heather and jade interior with copper flourishes. SUP and kayak hire is available with Seasports Southwest (*seasports-sw.com*), which also offers a variety of guided trips and courses with instructors, upriver or around the seafront (*gopaddling.info/rivers/river-teign*).

NORTH DEVON

The tidal River Torridge, which passes through Bideford and connects with the River Taw at Appledore before tumbling out into the Bristol Channel, is one of North Devon's calmer places to paddle in an area famous for its big surf waves. Adventure Boardsports (*adventureboardsports.co.uk*) runs beginners' lessons and guided trips on the river, or around to the beach of Westward Ho! It's there that Kitemare (*surfandkiteshop.co.uk*) has SUP hire too. Options for afters include **The Royal George** (*trgpub.co.uk*) in Appledore, a nice 18th-century waterside pub, or next door neighbour **The Beaver Inn** (*beaverinn.co.uk*), with occasional live music. Also in north Devon, OSKC Watersports (*oskcwatersports.co.uk*) offers tours and hire from pretty Combe Martin, a protected bay, where the **Focsle Inn** (*focsleinn.co.uk*) has beer tables on the seafront.

RIGHT: The village of Appledore, where the River Torridge and River Taw meet (photo: iStock).

The South

Dorset

9 Christchurch and Avon Loop

- 7km (4.3 miles)
- Lively, fun, challenging
- Tidal river
- Out and back
- No licence needed

Lively waterside pubs and bars, armadas of sailing dinghies and yachts, little leisure motorboats puttering up and down, SUP and kayakers having a ball, maybe the odd swimmer – this super-fun section of tidal river hosts more waterborne action than you could shake a paddle at. It's a great place to get stuck in to river life in all its forms.

Lying just a few kilometres east of Bournemouth, and pretty much blending into it, Christchurch is a vibrant town in a great location between the New Forest and the Solent. Two rivers meet within it, the broad Stour and narrower Avon. Between the two on the riverfront is the beautiful tall-spired 11th-century Priory Church, one of the only monasteries to get through the reign of Henry XIII unscathed.

Paddling downriver to Christchurch Harbour, which is partly enclosed by Mudeford's sandy spit, is an option but a challenge – the currents at the far end can be tricky and experts who like playing in whitewater often head here. Heading upriver is far easier, though it gets busy with day boaters when the sun shines.

BELOW: The start of the Avon Loop in Christchurch.

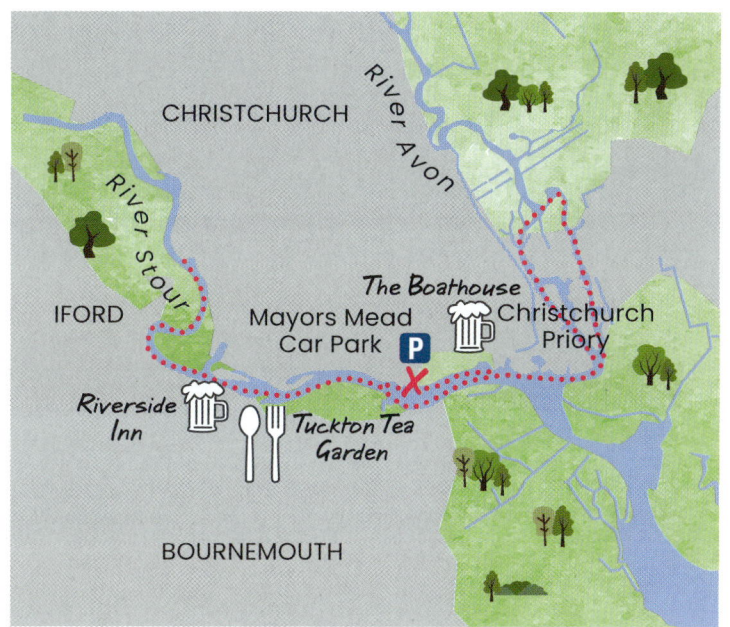

When I paddleboarded here on a hot day, my balance was seriously tested by the bumpy wash caused by the constant passing of motor boats. Still, it's a great, fun route, and we all need to improve our balance, right?

Start from the jetty beside the huge Mayors Mead car park in the centre, where it's easy to inflate on the grass, then head north up the River Stour, going as far as you like.

On the left, you will soon come to Tuckton Tea Gardens, which offers motorboat hire. Is it too early for a coffee and a cake? Beside it are jetties and grassy banks where you can moor up on your return to visit **The Riverside pub**. You can't paddle right up to it, so leave your SUP or kayak here, and cross the road on foot to reach it. A smart terrace above the water will tempt you to spend longer than you planned, while the interior is slick and modern (it's a cool-wallpaper-in-the-loos sort of place).

After the pub, continue downstream back into Christchurch and into the wider part of the river towards the harbour, for the second part of your paddle: a clockwise spin of the Avon Loop on the River Avon. This short circular through the town is often fast flowing and feels as entertaining as a theme park ride, with tight bends and low bridges to negotiate. It can be a little zippy and turbulent in parts, depending on recent rainfall

ABOVE: The well-stocked bar of The Boathouse.

CLOCKWISE FROM TOP LEFT: A refreshing pint at The Riverside; a water view of the Stour; the terrace of The Riverside; one of Christchurch's pretty bridges.

Having completed the circuit as many times as you like, paddle back upstream past the town quay and the grassy area called The Quomps to ditch your kit at the start point, and head over to **The Boathouse**. This big stylish bar near the waterfront has a party atmosphere and a menu of arancini, poke bowls, scallops, meze and more. The cocktail list runs to watermelon margaritas and negroni bianco. Enjoy.

▶ Details

For the venues, see (*bournemouthboating.co.uk/tuckton-tea-gardens*), (*theriversidebournemouth.co.uk*) and (*boathouse.co.uk*). Hire SUPs, arrange lessons and tours, or sign up your children to group classes with The SUP School (*thesupschool.co.uk*) in Christchurch; Shore Sports (*shoresports.co.uk*) hires out SUPs and kayaks from Mudeford Quay and runs guided trips up to the Priory. Buy locally-made SUPs, paddles and more at Christchurch store Avon Beach SUP (*avonbeachsup.co.uk*).

For information on the routes and area, see the tourist board's website (*visit-dorset.com/blog/post/the-delights-of-christchurch*).

▶ Make a weekend of it

The 67-room Harbour Hotel and Spa (*harbourhotels.co.uk/christchurch*) is next to Mayors Mead so couldn't be better placed, with two smart restaurants, an expansive terrace and waterside garden.

BELOW: The banks of the River Stour north of Christchurch.

Hampshire

10 Beaulieu River to the Yachtsman's Bar

- 3.2 km (2 miles)
- Historic, tranquil, leafy
- Tidal river
- Out and back
- Licence needed

If there can be such a thing as a 'luxury paddle', that's what this experience feels like.

Drifting up and down a gorgeous, calm tidal stretch of the Beaulieu River, you'll pass through the grounds of the Beaulieu Estate, discover a yachties' paradise and stop off at two posh enclaves, each with a fabulous historic pub.

Everything here looks as perfect as a film set, from the wooded banks to the elegant red-brick buildings of the pubs, smart and polished, swathed in wisteria and overlooking the harbour.

At only 19.3km (12 miles) in total, the river is short and sweet. Beaulieu village and the Beaulieu Estate's abbey, palace and motor museum are at the northern, inland end, and at the southern, via many wiggling meanders, is the Solent. About halfway up is Buckler's Hard, a village home to Buckler's Hard Yacht Harbour, and the famous ship-building site where three of Nelson's naval vessels were constructed, and where innumerable yachties have flocked to moor and explore ever since.

Built in the 1720s by the 2nd Duke of Montagu, it was intended

BELOW: The upper end of the Beaulieu River.

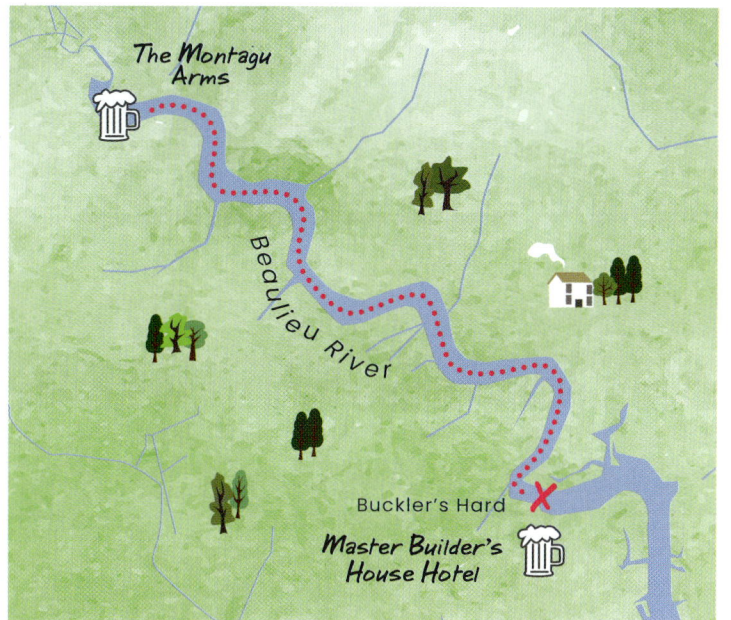

to be called Montagu Town and serve as a free port for the West Indies sugar trade. However, the duke's enterprises failed and in the 1740s the Navy turned it into a civilian shipyard. The yard's first overseer, Henry Adams, built an attractive red-brick house beside the harbour, now the Master Builder's House Hotel, whose atmospheric **Yachtsman Bar** is where you'll finish up for that well-earned thirst-slaker.

The catch with the Beaulieu River is that unlike other tidal rivers, which belong to the crown, it's privately owned (some quirk of a deal done in Henry VIII's era), so you'll need to pay the fee at the harbour office to launch if you're coming under your own steam. At this midway point there's a car park, and easy access to the water. It's also a nature reserve so you can't stop along the banks and must stay clear of wildlife and birds.

Because the river is tidal, the upper reaches are only accessible at high tide – the Solent means there's a double high tide, due to funky currents caused by proximity to the Isle of Wight, but it empties in one fast flow. So check those tide times.

A stress-free way to see the river is on a tour by open Canadian-style canoe or kayak with New Forest Activities (operated by Liquid Logistics). These depart from Bailey's Hard, north of Bucklers, on the west bank, which is reached through

ABOVE: A glass of the Montagu Arms's own lager is a refreshing reward.

CLOCKWISE FROM TOP LEFT: Book a Canadian-style canoe tour from Buckler's Hard; the leafy Montagu Arms; exploring a side creek of the Beaulieu River on a Liquid Logistics tour; the village of Beaulieu.

woods from the Liquid Logistics centre and car park. Tour options include 'family paddling', a 'river explorer' trip, 'sunset chasers', and themed paddles, such as a Halloween special. Up to Beaulieu and back is just over 3km (2 miles). There's also a 'paddle to the pub' one-way trip ending at **The Master Builders**, which is 2.7km (1.7miles), or one from Bucklers Hard to Beaulieu and back (10km/6 miles). I found paddling here utterly enchanting and relaxing, especially as I stayed longer afterwards for a delicious river swim.

It's not possible to tie up at the jetty in Beaulieu village at the north end without permission, but return later to visit the smart half-timbered **Montague Arms**. Polished, clad in wisteria, with a blissful garden overflowing with fragrant honeysuckle, lilies and mahonia out the back, this posh hotel also has a sleek wood-panelled bar. **Monty's Inn** serves excellent bar food such as salt-baked beetroot with blue cheese, truffle chips, and Brixham plaice fish-finger sandwich. A creative fine-dining restaurant, The Terrace, is another option if you're not going to drip river water all over the floor.

Back down the other end, stay longer at the Master Builder's House Hotel for drinks and crisps in the low, wood-beamed Yachtsman Bar, or at tables on the long luscious lawn leading to the water. There's modern British pub food (flat iron steak, New Forest pork chop) at Henry's, which is better than its smarter Riverview restaurant, but, in my experience, you're best to eat up at the Montagu Arms.

It's worth a potter around the village; the old New Inn pub is now a visitors' centre, and there are lovely waterside walks.

ABOVE: The bar and wine selection at Monty's Inn.

▶ Details

Arrange canoe tours through New Forest Activities (*newforestactivities.co.uk/canoeing*). Find information about: the marina and launching at (*beaulieuriver.co.uk*); the route at (*gopaddling.info/rivers/river-beaulieu*); the area at (*newforestnpa.gov.uk*).

▶ Make a weekend of it

The Montagu Arms (*montaguarmshotel.co.uk*) has luxurious rooms and garden cottages; while The Master Builder's House Hotel (*themasterbuilders.co.uk*) has gorgeous rooms, primped up with fine red flowery throws, plus three cottages.

Hampshire

11   River Hamble: Botley Brewery's Hidden Tap

- 3–5km (2–3 miles)
- Quirky, secret
- Tidal river
- Out and back
- No licence needed

Oh, this is a good one! Possibly my favourite, and certainly the most quirky. It involves a hidden creek, only accessible at high tide, and a place to order your drink straight to your board or kayak, lowered down to you after you've rung a bell dangling on a string and shouting up your order. **The Hidden Tap** is genius.

This beer pilgrimage takes place on the tidal River Hamble, a baby river of 10km (6.3 miles) that rises in Bishop's Waltham and flows to Southampton Water, towards the Solent.

Park in the car park at Burridge Recreation ground next to the Burridge Village Hall on the east side of the river (free at time of publication but please check). Follow the footpath for five minutes from the back of the sports fields through pretty woods to the river, where a small beach attracts swimmers and muck-about paddlers. Further down, currents are powerful, and even here there's quite a pull, but heading upstream it's soon altogether gentler, becoming narrower and shallower. Set off at least two hours before high tide. Creeks off to the sides turn to mud at low tide. That's something to bear in mind if you're considering a stop on Curbridge Creek, at the lively **Horse and Jockey**, which offers a big beer garden rolling down to it. Keep a wawry eye on the tide if

BELOW: Easy paddling on the River Hamble.

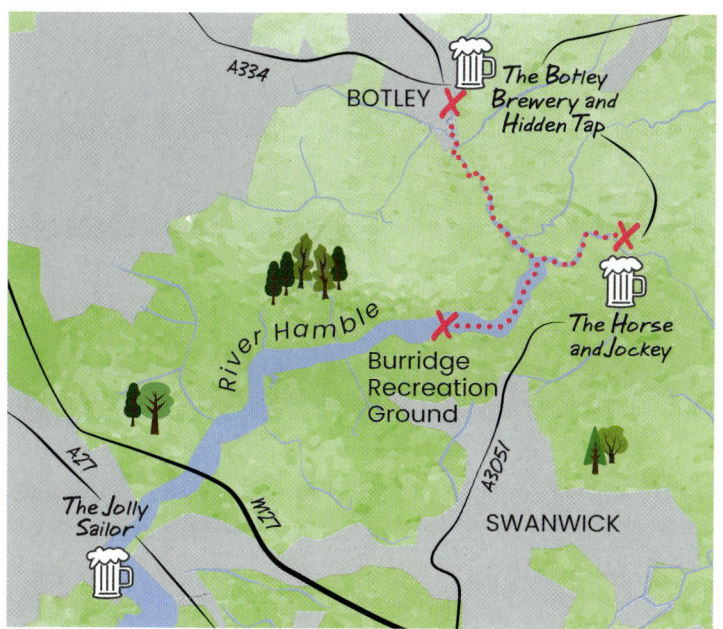

you're pushing to fit in both venues, as you need the high tide to reach them. On the Hamble you get a double tide, due to the way the tide bounces off the Isle of Wight – check timings.

En route, I saw white egrets and colourful geese, fish flopping and plopping at the surface, and the occasional paddler relaxing on their board.

Following the river as it curves west towards Botley, you'll pass YMCA Fairthorne on the right, which has a cafe. As Botley appears along the banks, the channel narrows and darkens where trees overhang. The Hamble's creeks feel like an otherworldly bayou.

Above the section of river navigable by boats, I rounded a bend to find an open, sun-dappled pool. A group of teenagers in bikinis and board shorts were hanging out on their boards in front of a small bridge, waiting for high tide so they could push their boards through the tunnel to the Botley Brewery. I happily joined them. Once we had crawled through, we queued at the foot of the brewery wall to ring the bell and hear what was on offer today – a citrusy IPA named 'Citra Ass Down', or an amber blonde beer by the name of 'Pommy Blonde'. An excellent fresh pint was lowered down in a wooden box, along with a card reader. You sip on your SUP, then return (unless you've arranged for someone to collect you in Botley). A unique pub paddle experience!

ABOVE: The Botley Brewey's Hidden Tap bar will lower beers down to paddlers.

CLOCKWISE FROM TOP LEFT: Pull to order your drink; the queue for the bar; the Horse and Jockey's beer garden on Curbridge Creek.

▶ Details

Hire beginners' and touring paddleboards, kayaks and double kayaks from The Paddle Centre (*thepaddlecentre.co.uk*) in Swanwick, which also offers tuition and guiding; or from YMCA Fairthorne (*ymca-fg.org/fairthorne-manor/river-access*), which provides coaching. The SUP Company (*thesupco.com*) has a test centre on the nearby Itchen, to try before you buy. For the pubs, see (*horseandjockey.pub*) and (*botleybreweryltd.com/hidden-tap*).

▶ Make a weekend of it

Moored at Cabin Boatyard on the river, Hamble River Beds (*hambleriverbeds.co.uk*) is a smart houseboat sleeping four. Mansion at Coldeast (*coldeastmansion.co.uk*), a revamped Victorian mansion hotel in Sarisbury near the river, has manicured grounds and a restaurant.

▶ Alternative routes

There's a put-in at YMCA Fairthorne (*ymca-fg.org*), where you pay to launch your own craft, or hire one. It has a cafe, activities such as talks and ziplines, as well as a campsite.

On the west side of the river, launch from the River Hamble Country Park (*hants.gov.uk*), which has a car park and cafe, playgrounds and crabbing from a jetty. Visible from the jetty is the wreck of a medieval naval vessel of King Henry V, the Grace Dieu. Built from 1416–18 in Southampton, it was huge and heavy for its time. It is thought that her maiden voyage ended in a disastrous mutiny at the Isle of Wight over her seaworthiness. Laid to rest in a mud berth on the Hamble in 1434, she was then decimated in a fire. At the time, the fire's origin was blamed on a lightning strike, though it was rumoured to have been started by the shipkeeper minding her, who stole and sold off her parts then started the fire to cover up his crime. The park also has the ruined buildings of HMS Cricket, which housed crew involved in the D-Day landings.

Another start point is Swanwick, where you can hire from the Paddle Centre at Premier Marina Swanwick (*thepaddlecentre.co.uk*), before a half-mile paddle to the waterside red-brick pub dating to 1751, **The Jolly Sailor** (*jollysailoroldbursledon.co.uk*) in Bursledon, which has a pontoon, outdoor terrace and an art-filled interior with old beams. Those up for it could do the whole route from here to Botley.

12 Chichester Harbour: Itchenor to the Crown and Anchor

West Sussex

- 9.7km (6 miles)
- Coast, seafood, nature
- Tidal estuary
- Out and back
- Harbour launch fee

Sometimes a paddle is so dazzlingly fresh and joyful, it lodges in the memory as sunbeams and sparkles. That's what this route through the natural Chichester Harbour felt like when I followed it on a good-weather day, sunshine glinting on the gentle wash of the tidal channel flowing to the Solent at West Wittering to the west.

About halfway up from the sea on the south side is the small harbour of Itchenor, on the Manhood Peninsula. It has a public slipway, which is the start point for an uplifting paddle to the smart and foodie waterside pub, the **Crown and Anchor** at Dell Quay.

Look out for cormorants, plover, terns and little egrets, as you head upriver with the incoming tide, working up an appetite as you paddle towards your seafood lunch at around high tide. Ride the tide back out afterwards.

It's about two hours there and back, and you may well want to linger a little longer if going under your own steam, rather than a group excursion, as it's a fabulous pub.

I recommend the guided small group trip with Fluid Adventures, not least because you can borrow a razor-sharp sea kayak that slices through the water, making you realise what you've been missing in your inflatable. A tour on a tidal estuary such as this is a great introduction to sea kayaking, far easier than heading out into the sea.

BELOW: Heading east on a Fluid Adventures tour.

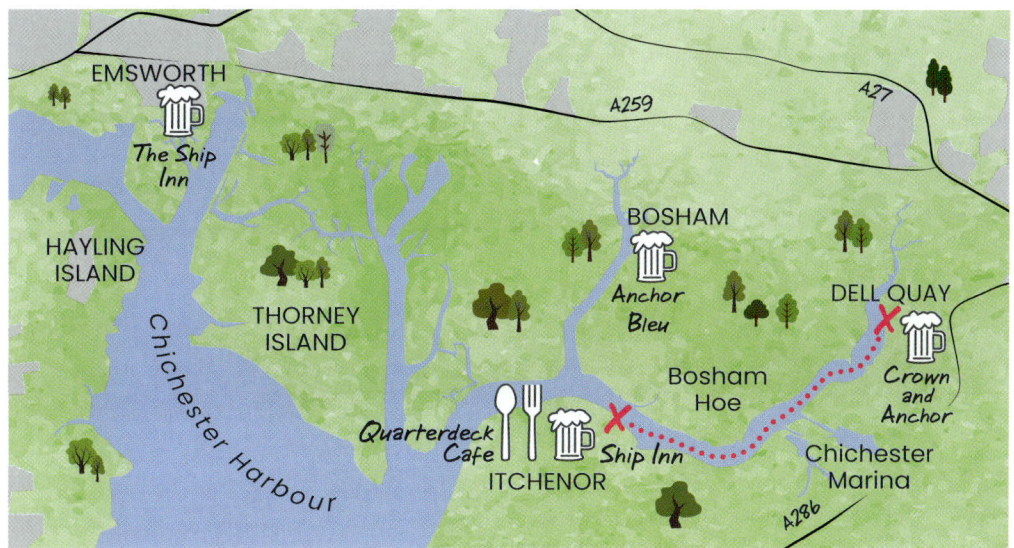

My guide, Andy Ironside, led the way, giving guidance and suggesting practice loops before we set out in convoy east, a light spray of salt-water sprinkling our cheeks. We passed through an armada of anchored yachts and dinghies, then followed the curve of the channel, playing 'which mansion would you choose' as we paddled by the private Bosham Hoe estate.

The entry to Birdham Pool Marina, which leads to the Chichester Canal, precedes the posh Chichester Marina.

Eventually there's a stretch of mud outside the pub, and you can pull in. Remember to drag the vessel right up the beach, or else, as one local shouted to a group of youngsters about to abandon theirs too early: 'they won't be here when you come back from the pub!'

Perhaps they wouldn't care. This glorious 16th-century inn is a place to linger, especially on a warm day when the waterside terrace, with several levels and corners to hide away in, comes into its own. The vibe is a bit boaty, a tad young and lively, and all in all a happy spot for a plate of seafood. Go for a simple two pint option – one of prawns, one of beer (Youngs is on tap, plus Beavertown Neck Oil), or try the scallops, day boat fish, haddock and chips, chowder or crab thermidor – local and excellent.

Friday evenings mean oysters, served with a dry white from the local Tinwood winery.

The relaxed return paddle to Itchenor should feel a doddle

BELOW: A pint of prawns and a pint of Neck Oil in the sunny Crown and Anchor.

12 CHICHESTER HARBOUR

CLOCKWISE FROM TOP LEFT: A bowl of mussels at the pub; the Crown and Anchor's exterior (photo: the Crown and Anchor); the view from the pub dining room; pulling kayaks up to ensure they're still there after lunch.

as long as you keep an eye on timings to go with the tide.

Back on dry land, wander through the pleasant boatyard to the **Quarterdeck Cafe**, which serves beer and cocktails, coffee, sarnies and ice cream, or perhaps up the road to the friendly **Ship Inn**.

▶ Details

The public Chichester Harbour Conservancy Car Park is a short way up the hill from Itchenor, where you can put in if you pay harbour fees (*conservancy.co.uk/on-the-water/paddlesports*). Fluid Adventures (*fluidadventures.co.uk/tours/chichester-pub-paddle*) offers hire and tours, including this 'Chichester Harbour Pub Paddle', which they class as 'easy'. A ferry runs between Itchenor and Bosham. For pubs see (*crownandanchorchichester.com*), (*quarterdeckcafe.co.uk*) and (*theshipinnitchenor.co.uk*).

▶ Make a weekend of it

The Ship Inn (*theshipinnitchenor.co.uk*) has spick and span rooms, or in Bosham, try the Millstream Hotel and Sea School Restaurant (*millstreamhotel.com*) with rooms and self-catering apartments.

▶ Alternative route

Explore some of the western channels of the natural Chichester Harbour, paddling up to Boshun to the family-run **Anchor Bleu** pub (*anchorbleu.co.uk*), which serves local beers such as a pilsner from the Fauna Brewery in West Sussex. Fluid Adventures offers this as a two-hour trip. Or try a gentle paddle on the Chichester Canal (buy a licence at *chichestercanal.org.uk/attractions/canoeing*); book a lesson there with Surfs Sup Watersports (*surfs-sup.co.uk*).

Those who know what they're doing might go west, around Thorney Island and up to **The Deck** (*thedeckcafeemsworth.co.uk*), a waterside restaurant at Emsworth Yacht Harbour in Emsworth.

Beyond that is Hayling Island. Surfs Sup Watersports offers SUP lessons here. On the mainland shore, on the north side of Sweare Deep in Langstone, the Fuller's pub **The Ship Inn** (*shiplangstone.co.uk*) is a former mill with cask ales, benches overlooking the water and seaview tables indoors.

BELOW: The lively beer garden at the Crown and Anchor.

Hampshire

13 Basingstoke Canal: to Odiham's The Waterwitch

- 4.4km (2.75 miles) one-way
- 8.9km (5.5 miles) return
- Countryside, history, gentle
- Canal
- Out and back or one way with pickup
- Licence needed

If 'canal' makes you think 'shopping trolley and floating carrier bags' then take a trip to this leafy waterway to realise how wrong you can be. In summer, the banks are high with flowers and grass, bees buzz and the water is dappled with sunlight. It is as quiet and untarnished as a remote river. Paddlers love it in autumn too, when red and amber reflections colour your watery way.

The Basingstoke Canal runs for over 50km (32 miles) between West Byfleet in Surrey and Greywell in Hampshire.

This stretch has a pub and a car park at both ends, so if there are two of you, leave a car at Odiham, at the car park near Colt Hill Bridge. Go in one direction from there, starting from right beside the car park next to the simple **Barley Mow** pub, Winchfield.

On a late summer's day I followed this route with a family friend, Sega, who had handily just completed a course to teach paddleboarding, so I enjoyed picking up some tips on technique as we went along, enjoying our peaceful journey.

From Winchfield the gentle route passes under a few canal bridges, and after 4.5 km (2.8 miles), you'll reach **The Waterwitch**, a real country charmer of a pub. Get out on the other side of the bridge and leave your kayak there, or do as we did and carry your SUP up to the pub's grassy garden. The garden nudges against the canal but there's no direct water access. Inside, this cosy pub still has its 17th-century beams and fireplaces for chilly days, but if it's warm, the garden is a delightful place to hang out with a cool drink or cup of tea. Cask ales and the usual sort of pub grub are on offer.

Paddle a little further then clamber out to have a look at the imposing ruin of King John's castle, built in 1207 as one of just three fortresses constructed during his reign. It's just north of Odiham, in the enclave of North Warnborough, where you can leave the canal and walk up Hook Road to another fantastic pub, the Grade II listed **Mill House**. There were once eight millhouses in the village according to the Domesday book of 1086. This last remaining one now has beautiful gardens and lawns laid around the millpond, with a working water wheel inside the smart, wood-panelled interior. The food here is more interesting than the usual: beef shin

BELOW: Outside the Mill House pub.

THE SOUTH

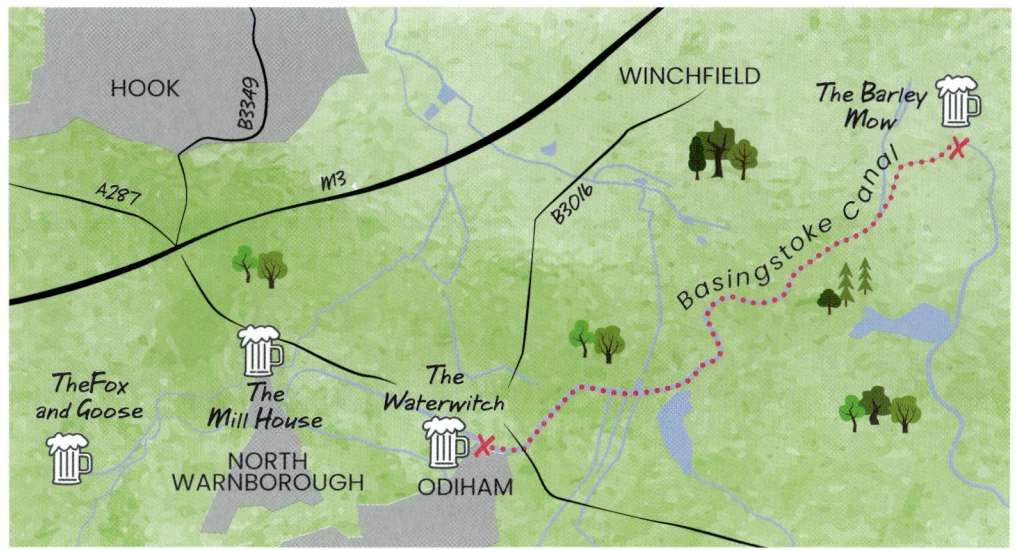

tortellini, tandoori halloumi burger and more. If you've left a car in Odiham, get out there, else it's time to turn around for the paddle back.

▸ Details

For the pubs, see (*chefandbrewer.com*) for The Waterwitch (*brunningandprice.co.uk/millhouse*) and (*barleymowwinchfield.co.uk*). For more information, see the Basingstoke Canal Society's site (*basingstoke-canal.org.uk/paddling*) and Paddle UK's (*gopaddling.info/canals/basingstoke-canal*) for more options along the canal. Hire kayaks and SUPS in summer at the Canal Centre in Mytchett (*basingstoke-canal.org.uk/the-canal-centre-mytchett*), which also has a campsite.

▸ Make a weekend of it

By the towpath in Greywell, just west of Odiham, the **Fox and Goose** pub (*facebook.com/foxandgoosegreywell*) has a camping ground (*ukcampsite.co.uk*).

▸ Alternative routes

Elsewhere on the canal, in Ash Vale, cosy pub **The Swan** (*chefandbrewer.com*) makes for a pretty stop, with flowery wallpaper and wood beams. There's a car park and a put-in at Ash Vale Railway Bridge by the station.

BELOW: Practising SUP skills on the nice calm Basingstoke Canal.

Oxfordshire/Gloucestershire

14 Upper Thames: Buscot to Lechlade

- 4.8km (3 miles)
- Coastal, dramatic, cave
- River
- Out and back
- Licence needed

A fish's plop, waving reeds, a bird's call, and silence. Teenagers snoozing on a bank, or paddleboarding playfully as they drift around the curves of the somnolent river. Mature trees and empty golden fields. The sights and sounds around the upper part of the great river, near Faringdon and Lechlade-on-Thames, couldn't be more different to the busy thoroughfare of the capital. Some 40km (25 miles) down from here is Oxford, with its punts and boathouses. And 225km (140 miles) downstream are the famous bridges and buildings of the capital, the tourist speedboats and commuter ferries, the grime and the filth, and the history. But at the highest navigable part of the Thames are only herons, clear water, and a gentle breeze. It's a quiet and easy-flowing ribbon to delight in a lazy afternoon of paddling, and perhaps even swimming.

The Trout Inn has sat amongst it all for 800 years, if you count its origins as an almshouse in 1229. It was built to house workers constructing a stone bridge over the river to replace the wooden one. It was, and still is, dedicated to St John, and the pub has held the fishing rights to a stretch of river here almost since that time.

BELOW: The Riverside pub in Lechlade-on-Thames.

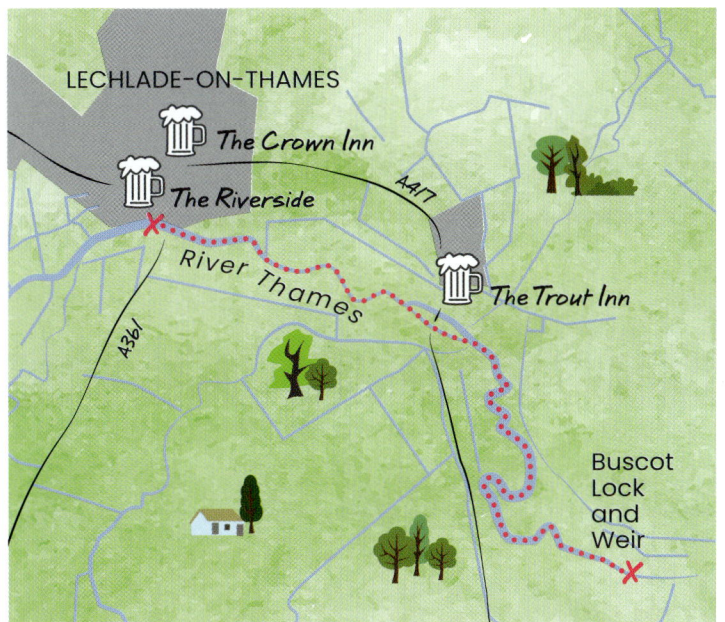

Nowadays it's a perfect example of a traditional Cotswold pub – but one without the celebrity chef at the helm and the greige-Scandi-rustic makeover. Landlady Penny Warren has run the place for three decades and kept it and its wood-floored interior as trad as can be, and it's all the better for it. A grandfather clock and a 7kg (15.5lbs) taxidermy pike, caught here in 1902, are as far as interior design goes. Expect friendly chat at the bar, a long-serving regular or two propping it up, and in summer, a garden full of life. People stop by for drinks in the marquee, then get caught up watching folk bands on stage outside beside the pop-up Creel Bar. The annual Riverfolk Festival in July is always a good show.

To experience it, independent paddlers can follow a gorgeous leafy route starting just over a kilometre (less than a mile) mile downriver in the pretty village of Buscot. It's imperative to start with scones and tea in the garden of the little red-brick Buscot Village Tearoom (*facebook.com/buscot.tearoom*). You'll need your strength as there's about a 15-minute (1km/half-mile) portage from the village car park, along a well-marked footpath, through fields, past Buscot Weir (where locals dip) and over a lock bridge to get onto the river. Paddling upriver for about 30 minutes, the blue-brown flat-rippled water stretches wide to tree-lined banks at first, then twists into tighter gullies, and opens again near the

CLOCKWISE FROM TOP LEFT: Inside the Trout Inn; the Riverside; the garden of the Trout Inn; the bridge at Buscot weir; the peaceful Thames.

pub. On the way you'll pass Cheese Wharf, from where the finest local cheeses began their journey to London. The Trout's grassy beer garden sits above the waterline, with easy mooring.

An alternative is to hire gear around 1.5km (1 mile) upriver at Lechlade: Cotswold Canoe Hire is right next to **The Riverside**, a smart-funky pub with a beer garden and wild west-ish interiors. Also very cool, minutes from the river, is **The Crown Inn** with vintage decor, arcade games and a microbrewery.

▶ Details

Hire in Lechlade from Cotswold Canoe Hire (*cotswoldcanoehire. co.uk*). Go Paddling has excellent info on the Thames, including all the pubs (*gopaddling.info/rivers/river-thames*). For info about Buscot, see (*nationaltrust.org.uk/visit/oxfordshire-buckinghamshire-berkshire/buscot-village*). For the pubs, see (*thetroutinn.com*), (*riverside-lechlade.com*) and (*facebook.com/ thecrownlechlade*).

▶ Make a weekend of it

In Lechlade, **The Riverside** (*riverside-lechlade.com*) pub has neat bedrooms. Buscot Manor, near the lock, can be rented and sleeps 20, with paddleboards and bikes supplied. Nearby, the National Trust's Lock Cottage (*nationaltrust.org.uk/holidays/oxfordshire-buckinghamshire-berkshire/lock-cottage*) sleeps two. Lakes By Yoo (*thelakesbyyoo.com*) is a luxurious and active resort of contemporary holiday homes, with a spa and swimming lakes, just west of Lechlade.

ABOVE: A boat on the Thames near the Trout Inn.

LEFT: Kayak hire outside the Riverside pub.

More great paddles on the Upper Thames

THE RIVER THAMES: ONE LONG AND MIGHTY PUB CRAWL

Where do you start with the Thames? The UK's defining, capital-slicing and mighty river has shaped the country and its history, literature and cultural scene, its industries and tourism, arguably more than any other. Bubbling up merely as spring waters at Thames Head in Gloucestershire, it steadily gains strength to weave for 346km (215 miles) through the south, the home counties and the great city of London, to its gaping mouth at the North Sea. It is the longest river in England, and the second longest in the country. Navigable for most vessels up to Lechlade it has a joyous multitude of pubs all along the way, including some of the poshest, foodiest, oldest and most charming in the land. These are pubs imbued with history – in spots where ferryboats once carried folk over water before there were bridges, where Henry VIII hunted, where the old peddlers of wool and cheese took their respite. To paddle the whole river would be a phenomenal

BELOW: Messing about in the Thames near Wargrave.

undertaking, but possible in a week if you go for it. Lovelier though, perhaps, is to break it into shorter sections and tackle it as a long-term project, bit by bit. On the other hand, you could just pick one of these pubs and mess about on the water nearby, where the only challenge is choosing what to eat and drink afterwards. Here are a few ideas of routes and stops...

THE UPPER THAMES – BETWEEN LECHLADE AND OXFORD

Upriver from pretty Lechlade-on-Thames, there are a couple more pubs to paddle to, before the river becomes inaccessible for boaters. **The Red Lion** (*theredlioncastleeaton.co.uk*) in Castle Eaton has a riverside garden with a 'boho tent' for drinks and music, as well as shepherd hut accommodation. There's also the **White Hart Inn** (*thewhitehartashtonkeynes.com*) in Ashton Keynes, within the Cotswold Water Park (*waterpark.org*), a leisure park with lakes, accommodation and watersports.

Downriver from Lechlade, within a few kilometres, is **The Plough** (*theploughinnkelmscott.com*) in Kelmscott, a smart white-washed stone pub with bare stone walls and neutral-chic bedrooms. **Ye Olde Swan** (*yeoldeswan.co.uk*), a bit further on in Radcot, is situated next to the Thames's oldest bridge, used originally for pack horses transporting wool between Northampton and Southampton. The pub now has tipi glamping and camping. Down from there is the popular Oxfordshire pub, **The Trout at Tadpole Bridge** (*butcombe.com/the-trout-at-tadpole-bridge-oxfordshire*), hidden away in a remote spot, which has smart bedrooms.

OXFORD TO READING

The Oxford to Reading section is 69km (43 miles) of well-used river, full of villages and pubs frequented by city folk. Several operators offer kayak and SUP tours in the city of Oxford itself, which take in colleges and meadows from the water. Oxford Kayak Tours (*oxfordkayaktours.com*) has four-hour trips, or Ultimate Canoe and Kayak (*ultimate-canoeandkayak.co.uk*) has several and can arrange two-day trips all the way to Reading. Between the two, the spots to stop at or just do a short paddle nearby are **The Swan in Streatley Coppa Club** (*coppaclub.co.uk/theswanatstreatley*), a 17th-century inn turned design hotel with an outdoor riverside gym and paddleboarding, and its sister venue **The Great House Coppa Club**, downriver in Sonning

BELOW: A quiet stretch near Lechlade-on-Thames.

MORE GREAT PADDLES ON THE UPPER THAMES

(*coppaclub.co.uk/thegreathousesonning*), with garden igloos. It'd be a fun way to spend a weekend, staying a night in each and paddling between them. Along the way, Pangbourne has several pubs such as **The Swan** (*swanpangbourne.co.uk*), with a waterside terrace. Then, past Sonning, just before super chic Henley, there are easy roadside put-ins at Wargrave, home to the straightforward **George and Dragon** (*stgeorgeanddragon.co.uk*), a nice option for a short trip, with lovely river swimming (if the Thames pollution allows it on the day).

THE POSH PUB CRAWL – HENLEY TO WINDSOR

Britain's poshest paddle? Could be this 37km (23 mile) stretch of the Thames, between Henley-on-Thames and Windsor. It will take you from the town of rowers to the town of the royals and Eton, with numerous chichi, foodie enclaves lining the millionaires' belt riverbanks in between. On weekends you'll see the great and the good lying back with a bottle of champagne in their luxury motorboats, or settling in for the afternoon at a famous foodie pub. You could paddle small sections or try the whole thing – a gourmet paddle tour perhaps – but you'd need to break it into two or three days at least (and pack something smart to wear).

Henley Canoe Hire (*henleycanoehire.com*) can get you started, whether you want to hire for an hour, for two days to get to Windsor, or six to paddle the whole Thames. Alternatively, a few miles downriver in Bisham, Moose Canoe and SUP Hire (*moosecanoehire.com*) has a great range of vessels, from giant SUPs, canoes and kayaks to electric Zen boats, also available for multi-day hire.

Continuing downriver, Marlow is home to the UK's first two-Michelin-star pub, **The Hand and Flowers** (*thehandandflowers.co.uk*), where Tom Kerridge's fine three-course lunch will set you back £175 per head. There are a few other pubs on streets north of the river, but on the banks the **Compleat Angler** (*macdonaldhotels.co.uk/compleat-angler/food-and-drink/riverside-restaurant*) is a famous Thames' boozer (also a four star hotel). It was one of the earliest tourist guesthouses that, even in Dickens' day, was at risk of over-tourism – he commented it was often fully booked by boating parties. Now, it's quite swanky with fine Indian dining at Atul Kochhar's Sindhu restaurant.

Next stop, **The Bounty** (*facebook.com/thebounty1*) in Bourne

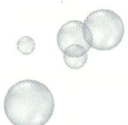

ABOVE: Riverside victuals in Henley (photo: iStock).

OPPOSITE: Paddleboarders pass weeping willows on the banks of the Thames near Goring and Streatley (photo: iStock).

RIGHT: A sunny day on the streets of Henley (photo: iStock).

End, a fun, piratey classic, only accessible on foot or by boat, with a wooden boat forming the bar inside an OTT interior decked in flags, fairy lights and boaty paraphernalia. **The Ferry** (*theferry.co.uk*) in Cookham is a decent smartened up option, so too **The Boathouse at Boulters Lock** (*boathouseboulterslock.co.uk*), on its own island in Maidenhead, which serves smart dishes on a riverview upper terrace. Taplow has the contemporary, airy **Hall and Woodhouse Taplow** (*hall-woodhousetaplow.co.uk*), with a wooden deck by the river next to moorings, though there's no direct access. Then you'll come to famously foodie Bray, home to Heston Blumenthal's Fat Duck, and The Waterside (*waterside-inn.co.uk*), a very smart, three-Michelin-star Alain Roux restaurant where there's an expectation to dress up. Soggy pants and muddy watershoes won't cut it at these, so you'll need to pack a shirt or dress in your dry bag.

Downstream, you'll paddle through the beautiful Cliveden Estate, which has canoes to rent for relaxed paddles among soaring trees, and Maidenhead, where Paddleboard Maidenhead (*paddleboardmaidenhead.uk*) goes beyond the normal hire and trips to offer sunset, yoga and full moon paddleboarding. As you near Windsor, more sightseeing boats will appear, and you could make a final stop at **The Boatman** (*boatmanwindsor.com*), overlooking Eton Bridge and serving an excellent Eton mess. I think we're all agreed that you've definitely earned it.

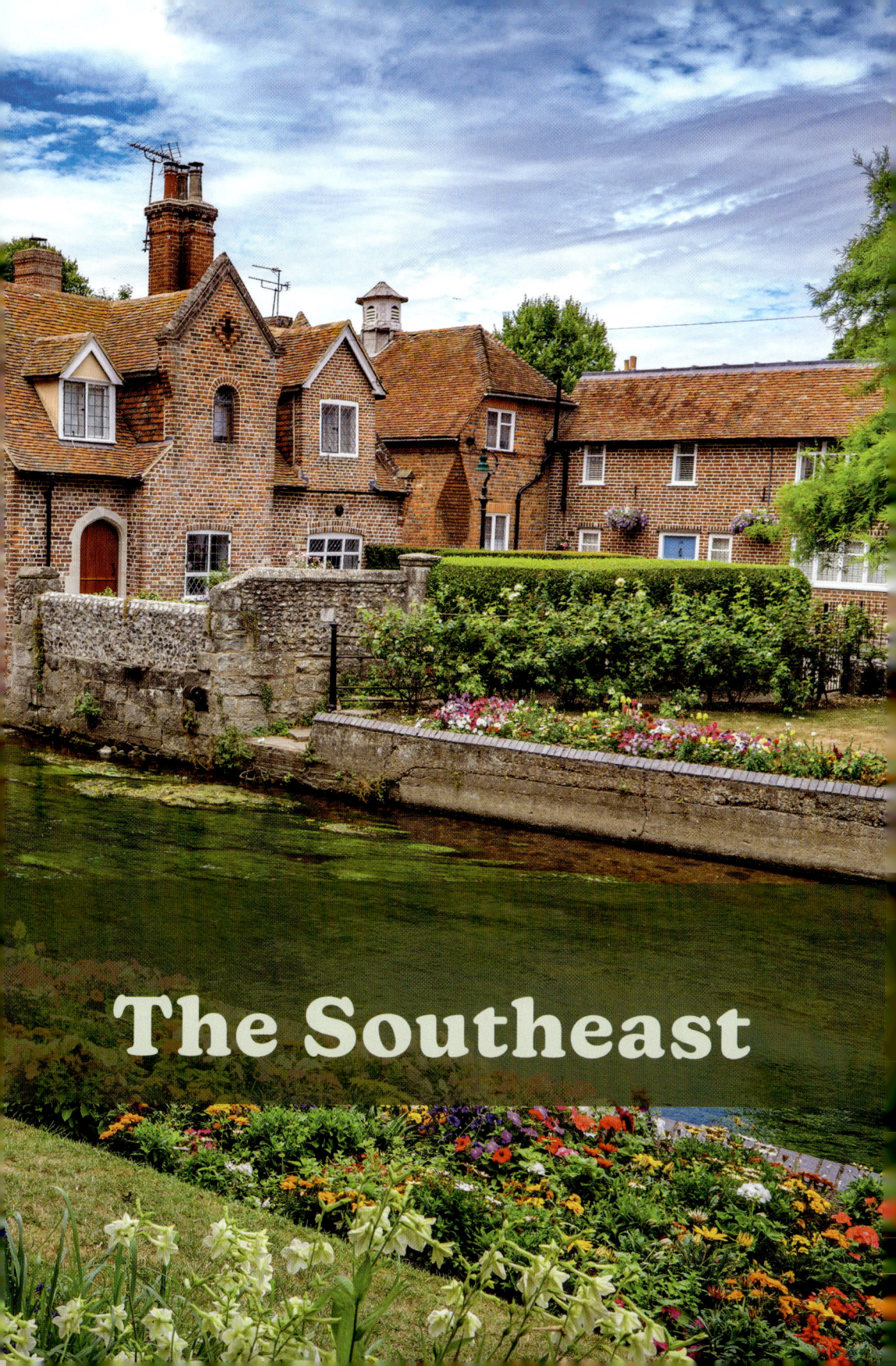
The Southeast

London

15 West London: Hurst Park to Richmond

- 12.9km (8 miles)
- History, culture, challenge
- River
- One way
- Licence needed

To see some of historic London and stop at one or two great old pubs, try this fun half-day paddle (or full day if you stop a lot), which passes Hampton Court Palace and ends at Richmond. Don't be intimidated by the mighty Thames, it's still fairly quiet and easy to negotiate here, though there are a few locks.

I did this route on a paddleboard, with my young kids and partner accompanying in an inflatable kayak, with no problem. Our start point was Hurst Park's Hurst Meadows car park (free at time of publication), where it's easy to enter the river. A relaxed five hours later, with one long stop for lunch, another for ice cream, we exited at Ham, where you (or one of you) could get a taxi or public transport back to your car.

From the suburb of Molesey, you'll pass Tagg's Island, where colourful houses and houseboats lining the shore will make you feel like you're in New England or Martha's Vineyard. Soon, on the left bank comes Hampton Court Palace, one of England's grandest and most significant sights, former seat of Henry VIII at the height of his powers and wealth – which is a thrill to see from the water! Just before the palace is a potential stop, **The Mitre**, a trendy boutique hotel whose Lion Terrace overlooks the river.

Keep paddling and next is **The Albany** at Thames Ditton, a popular spot with young cocktail-drinking couples, and a bit snazzy with its glass walled beer garden. I prefer the more characterful **Ye Olde Swan Inn**, which dates back to the 13th century and was once a Tudor hunting lodge used by Henry VIII. He built Thames Ditton island to aid his commute to the centre, and the pub is next to the island's iron bridge. Now it's a Greene King pub with a deck out back that makes for easy landing, and benches for a sunny pint.

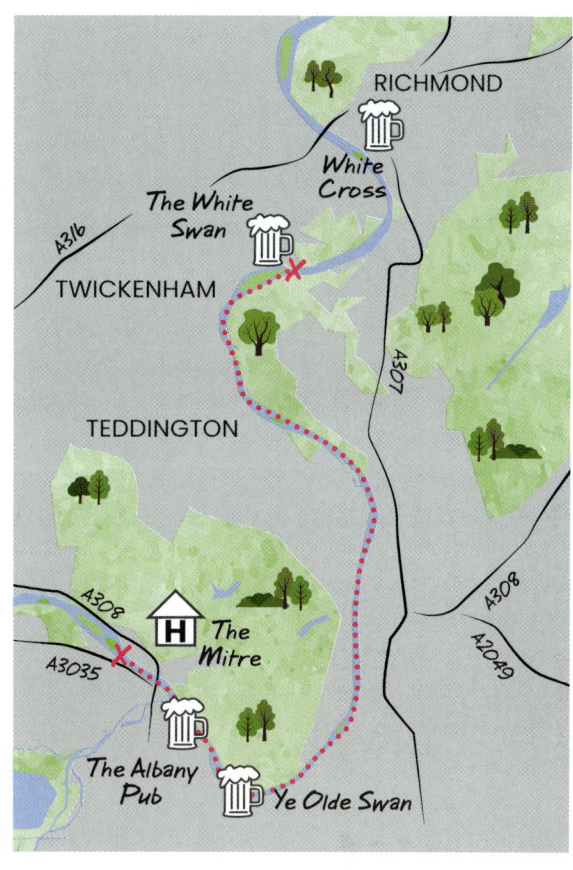

Passing through Surbiton and Kingston next, you'll see a few pubs and bars along the busy built-up banks, but it's best to wait until just past Eel Pie Island for the **White Swan Twickenham**. On rugby match days its terrace balcony and riverside gardens (which can flood at high tide) are packed with singing fans. A cosy 17th-century bar indoors has Harveys, Sharp's and Fuller's on tap. We ended near here on the right-hand bank at the Ham Street car park near Ham House.

Continue, and you'd pass through pretty Petersham, then Richmond, with its vast park of deer and the **White Cross Inn**, which proudly proclaims itself 'the pub that floods'. It makes a virtue of the fact that at high tide (the water rising up to 4.5m/14.8ft), drinkers can be cut off and stuck here, marooned on

OPPOSITE: The river Thames near Richmond.

15 WEST LONDON

CLOCKWISE FROM TOP LEFT:
A river exit near Ham; paddling the Thames into west London doesn't have to be daunting; riverside benches at Ye Olde Swan Inn at Thames Ditton.

their high bar seats. Wellies are available. No problem for paddlers of course, though you may like to have the excuse to stay put. Kew, Chiswick and Barnes, then Putney and Battersea follow if you carry on east, all with excellent, historic pubs of their own, though it's a busier bit of river as you head into the city.

▶ Details

For more info, see (*ukwaterwaysguide.co.uk/map/river-thames/main-channel*), (*gopaddling.info/rivers/river-thames*) and (*visitthames.co.uk*). Hampton Court Paddlesports (*hamptoncourtpaddlesports.com*) hires out SUPs, kayaks, canoes and giant SUPs in Mosely, just west of Hurst Park. Join excursions from Thames Ditton with Dittons Paddle Boarding (*dpbclub.co*). For the pubs, see (*mitrehamptoncourt.com*), (*the-albany.co.uk*), (*greeneking.co.uk/pubs/surrey/ye-olde-swan*), (*thewhitecrossrichmond.com*), (*whiteswantwickenham.co.uk*).

ABOVE: Paddling into Kingston.

LEFT: Taking in Hampton Court Palace from the water is a thrill.

More great paddles in London

EAST LONDON'S RIVER LEA, FROM THE MILK FLOAT TO THE PRINCESS OF WALES

Hackney Wick is a former industrial area in the east, now full of artists' studios. A decade ago it was all about underground warehouse raves, but now, inevitably, a wealth of bars and breweries have opened, drawing the crowds. It's here that Moo Canoes (*moocanoes.com*) runs one of London's best-known hire places next to a barge bar, **The Milk Float** (*themilkfloat.com*), which serves cocktails below deck and from a side hatch to those who paddle up. The most popular route is to head north along the River Lea to the **Princess of Wales** (*princessofwalesclapton.co.uk*) pub in Clapton, a very cool local spot with great brunches and roasts. Back near base, **The Crate Brewery** (*cratebrewery.com*) is the spot to go afterwards (and continue to the early hours if you like). Moo also has a base at Limehouse.

REGENT'S CANAL

The water might be mucky, but London life in all its varieties is strung along this important waterway, and it links some of the city's finest neighbourhoods: Primrose Hill, Camden, Kings Cross, Islington and Hackney. The best pubs along the way – of which there are many – include Islington's **The Narrowboat** (*thenarrowboatpub.com*), with a balcony over the water, interesting cocktails (*try the banoffee espresso martini*) and great roasts, and the fabulous **Palm Tree** (no website) in Mile End, a vintage east London boozer with gold palm tree wallpaper and a happy lack of tarting up. For equipment hire, try the Pirate Castle (*thepiratecastle.org/canoe*); or in Paddington, Active 360 (*active360.co.uk/paddington-basin*).

ABOVE: Kayaks and canoes for hire on the banks of the Regent's Canal (photo: iStock).

OPPOSITE: The River Lea (photo: iStock).

Kent

16 River Medway: from The Boathouse, Yalding

- 6.4km (4 miles)
- Rural, easy, historic
- River
- Out and back
- Licence needed

For east and south Londoners, the River Medway provides one of the closest places to the big smoke to paddle for a green and natural escape.

While a river rolling through a very populated part of Kent could never offer a true wilderness experience (this route passes under a noisy road and a railway line), it does comprise long sections where reeds and rushes grow high along the banks and the quiet sounds of the countryside are all you'll hear.

The 113km (70 miles) Medway links Maidstone and Tonbridge, winding from the Sussex High Weald and emptying into the River Thames Estuary at Sheerness. Over the centuries, the river has gone from natural watercourse to heavily used industrial thoroughfare, to somewhere primarily used for leisure.

It was once busy and bustling: as a Roman trade route hauling

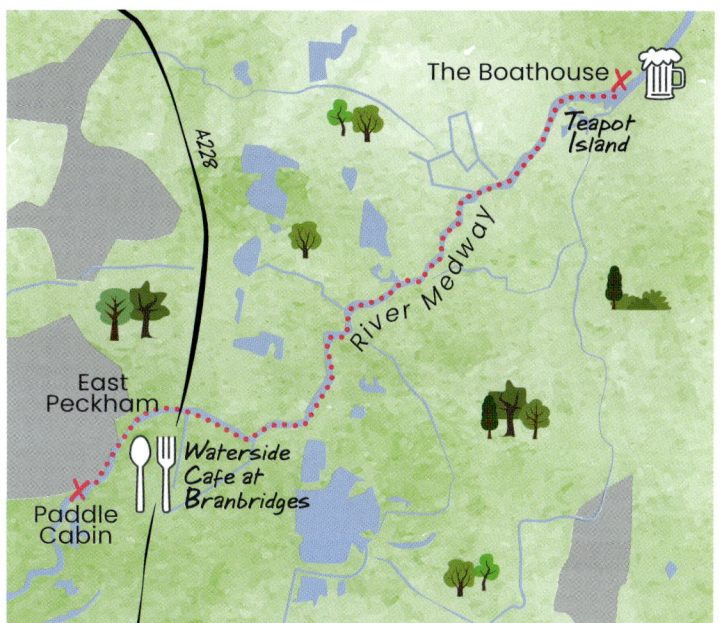

stone, and later for transporting paper, beer and timber. By the 18th century, when Maidstone was practically a glittering metropolis and the upper reaches were made navigable, it was a major trade river, though tidal, until locks were built – the first in 1792 at Allington.

These days, the Allington locks mark the end of a 29km (18 mile) River Medway Trail for paddlers, which starts in Tonbridge, once a capital of Kentish industry, and can be broken into sections. The short route I've pulled out is one of these sections, an out and back that takes in a popular pub for river users, **The Boathouse**, and which could easily be extended.

The start location is at Yalding Point, near to the massive grassy Lees Car Park, from where you can portage, crossing Twyford Bridge to use the Yalding Canoe Launch Point.

You'll pass a funny little place, **Teapot Island**, where a proper old-school caff has existed in some form since the 1950s. Back then, it sold bait to fishermen from a shack. Since 2003 it has housed an adjoining teapot exhibition with 8,500 different shaped teapots (clowns, cats, dragons, you name it) packed onto shelves as a perfect expression of English eccentricity.

Paddling east towards East Peckham, you'll relax as greenery explodes along the banks, kingfishers dart (I saw seven) and

OPPOSITE: A bridge over the Medway.

BELOW: A well-deserved post-paddle pint at The Boathouse.

16 RIVER MEDWAY 87

CLOCKWISE FROM TOP LEFT: DReeds and water lilies; The Boathouse pub outside and in; an oast house on the banks.

THE SOUTHEAST

waterlilies cover the surface. There is, I'm afraid, a grinding underpass to paddle beneath, and an iron rail bridge – bring your positivity and admire the graffiti.

After a few kilometres you'll come to a brilliant stop-off, **The Paddle Cabin**, a cool, forward-thinking outfit with SUP hire, tours and community paddle sessions shares a yard is the **Waterside Cafe at Branbridges**, which serves great coffee and cakes on a terrace under a weeping willow.

This is a good place to turn around and head back to the start point of Yalding. A pontoon at **The Boathouse** welcomes you, with a rack for paddles and SUPs. Inside, canoes are hung from the high wooden ceiling and boating paraphernalia scratches the surface of the pub's 600-year history. A century ago it was the end point for swimming races, although the water is probably not clean enough these days. Edith Nesbit, author of The Railway Children, stayed here, describing it as a place to 'be comfortable on the very lip of the river'. Renowned among paddlers, it has a great outdoor beer deck right on the water.

❯ Details

An official map of the River Medway Trail, with information, hire companies and camping spots can be found at tourist board website (*explorekent.org/wp-content/uploads/2016/05/CANOE_TRAIL_BOOKLET.pdf*). For the venues, see (*boathouseyalding.co.uk*), (*teapotisland.co.uk*) and (*facebook.com/watersidebranbridges*).

In the summer, you can hire in Yalding from Elveys Canoes (*elveys-canoe.co.uk*). The Paddle Cabin (*paddlecabin.co.uk*) offers paddleboard hire to do this route in reverse.

❯ Make a weekend of it

The Branbridges café site has a glamping tipi (*facebook.com/Branbridgesleisure*) in a separate garden, beside a field of goats, chickens and a playground.

❯ Alternative routes

The full River Medway Trail of 29km (18 miles) is a great challenge that takes two days, paddling downriver from Tonbridge to Allington Locks. The official map indicates places where you can wild camp.

Surrey

17 Wey Navigation: The Anchor

- 5.8km (3.6 miles)
- Countryside, gentle, suburban
- River navigation
- One way
- Licence needed

The River Wey's 17th-century navigation, owned by the National Trust, runs from the Thames at Weybridge to Godalming in Surrey. When joined with Godalming Navigation, they form a 32km (20 mile) navigable route taking in some of the county's pretty green scenery and towns.

It's a favourite place to get on the water for residents of this busy part of the south, and an easy escape from west London, just minutes off the M25 and close to Byfleet and New Haw railway station. Despite its busy surroundings, all the traffic chaos feels a million miles away once you're bobbing along among the herons, swans and dragonflies, undisturbed by anyone except the occasional barge.

Within a pleasant Surrey landscape, where the three villages of Pyrford to the north, Ripley to the east and Send to the west form a

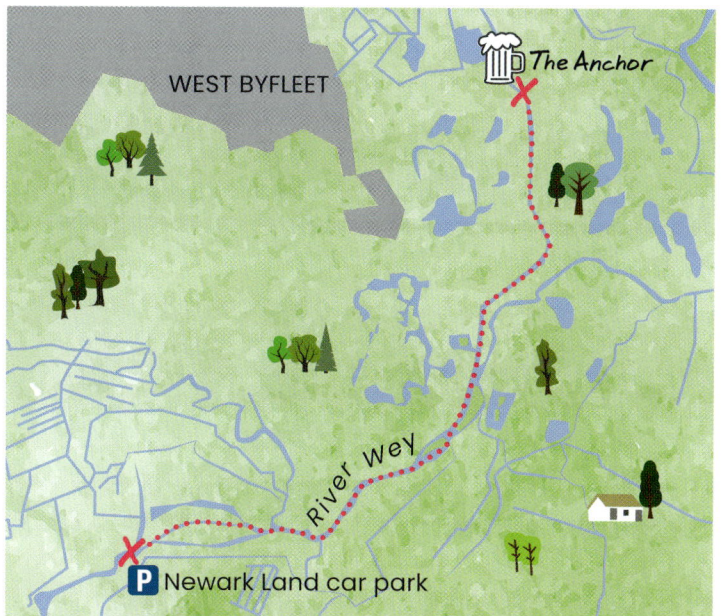

triangle, there's an easy starting place at Newark Lane Car Park, where you can easily access the river from big grassy fields. On a warm day there are usually wild swimmers, picnickers, paddlers and potterers with inflatables hopping on and off the banks.

Once you're in, the happy noises of other water users ebb away, and you'll pass under a bridge and alongside some red-brick buildings following a narrow, peaceful stretch of water north-east. As a navigation, the waterway has the feel of a canal. At Newark Lock you'll need to portage around. (Don't do what my daughter did and drop a paddle into the water, then have to lie on the grassy banks to retrieve it and get stung by a wasp.)

Keep to the right avoiding Ripley weir, but look out for the small square red-brick tower on the left – an Elizabethan summerhouse where the poet John Donne is believed to have lived between 1600 and 1604.

Eventually you'll come to Pyrford Lock, disembarking there just before **The Anchor**. This popular large modern venue has plenty of outdoor seating so prop your SUP against the wall or keep an eye on your kayak while you relax over a Dorset Badger Beer and pub grub such as nachos or mushrooms on toast.

At this point, someone will have to run back to get the car. That's what my partner and I often do – always packing some

OPPOSITE: Setting out on the Wey Navigation.

CLOCKWISE FROM TOP LEFT: Outside the pub; the calm waters of the Wey Navigation; the stretch beyond Newark Lock.

ABOVE: The riverside next to the Anchor pub.

running shoes in our dry bag. You might need to toss a coin to see who gets to enjoy the pint and who gets a work out and a drive. Otherwise take it easy as you'll have to paddle back to the start.

▶ Details

Find information about this route at the National Trust website (*nationaltrust.org.uk/visit/surrey/river-wey-and-godalming-navigations-and-dapdune-wharf/river-wey-information-for-canoeists*), including links to buy a day licence (otherwise covered by British Waterways annual licenses). For the pub, see (*anchorpyrford.co.uk*).

▶ Alternative route

About 10km (6 miles) south of the pub, Dapdune Wharf in Guildford is a good spot to get on the water, where Fluid Adventures (*fluidadventures.co.uk*) has SUPs and kayaks for hire. Guildford has a couple of waterside pubs, too. The Row Barge (*therowbargeguildford.com*) is a sports pub with a grassy beer garden right on the water that you could pull in at, as well as The Weyside (*theweyside.co.uk*), which is also right beside the water but fenced off without river access.

East Sussex

18 River Ouse: Barcombe Mills to The Anchor

- 3.2km (2 miles) or 16km (10 miles)
- Gentle, fun, easy
- River
- Out and back
- No licence needed

Deep in the East Sussex countryside, 8km (5 miles) north of the quirky town of Lewes, Barcombe Mills is a favourite day out for those living anywhere near, and especially cityfolk escaping Brighton or London for a hit of greenery and bucolic riverside bliss.

Flower-filled meadows and fields line the banks of the River Ouse, a narrow, pretty waterway that begins in West Sussex near Lower Beeding, flowing east then south and out to the Channel at Newhaven.

Point of call for many is **The Anchor Inn**, a lively, characterful pub dating to 1790 at Barcombe Mills, below which the river becomes tidal. The pub originally catered to horse-drawn barges, but these days the huge (and hopefully) sunny garden is typically full of children playing, scampering dogs, groups of cyclists and walkers, and families meeting for a pub lunch. There's an outdoor

94 THE SOUTHEAST

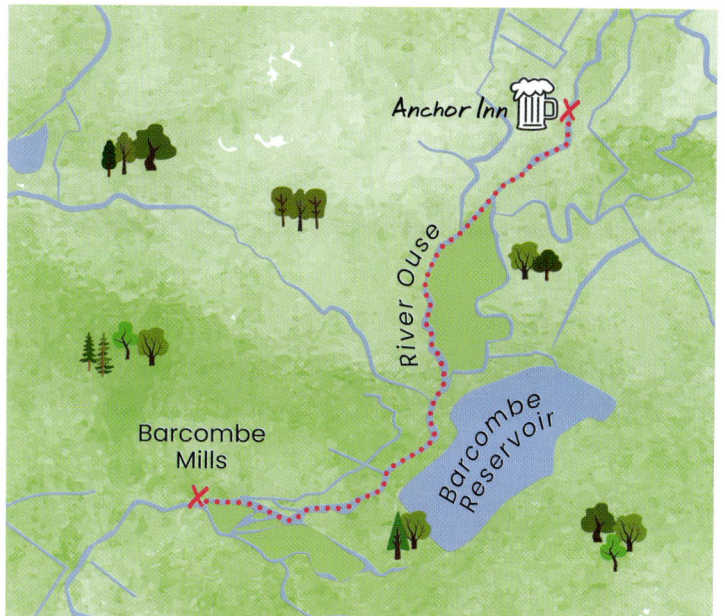

bar, but what sets it apart is having boats for hire – rowing boats, rather than paddle vessels, but they are great fun for a little muck about or to row upriver to the Fish River Falls. To paddle here properly you can come on a guided trip – some go all the way to Lewes – or visit independently. Get in further up or down stream to make your way here, and get out opposite the pub where a footpath runs to the bridge over it.

A good start point for a shorter paddle, a couple of kilometres (less than a mile) downstream from the pub, begins near the car park at Barcombe signposted 5km (3 miles) north of Lewes off the A26, turning right after the Cock Inn. A track from the car park leads to shallow launching spots.

For a longer paddle, go with the incoming tide from Lewes 8km (5 miles) to the south, getting onto the water near the **Harvey's Brewery** (shop and tours available). Do a 16km (10 miles) out and back, or come downriver from Barcombe to finish back in Lewes and relax at the diminutive **Snowdrop Inn** near the water, for cask ales and live music.

OPPOSITE: The Anchor Inn at Barcombe Mills.

▸ Details

To join a guided trip along the Ouse, try The Kayak Coach (thekayakcoach.com) and Hatt Adventures (thehatt.co.uk/

CLOCKWISE FROM TOP LEFT: The sunny back garden of the Anchor Inn; a misty morning on the River Ouse; paddling from the Boathouse Farm campsite.

kayaking-river-ouse). There's lots of information about the river and its system of streams and brooks at the website of the Ouse and Adur Rivers Trust (*oart.org.uk*); see info about paddling the river at Paddle UK's website (*gopaddling.info/rivers/river-ouse-in-sussex*). For the pubs, see (*anchorpyrford.co.uk*), (*facebook.com/thesnowdropinn*) and (*harveys.org.uk*).

◗ Make a weekend of it

A wonderful place to stay for paddlers who like camping is the Boathouse Farm campsite (*boathousefarm.co.uk*). A large field contains pitches right by the riverside, with easy launches just steps from your tent, facilitating dawn and sunset paddles. At the end of the season, in September, I was able to exclusively book the whole field with a group of friends; all had their own inflatable kayaks and SUPs, and we spent an idyllic weekend paddling down to the pub, loading our toddlers and beers onto boards to explore upriver, climbing onto rope swings and scrambling onto muddy banks.

The chocolate box village of Firle, also home to the Bloomsbury set home of Charleston Charleston, is a wonderful non-paddle at the foot of the Downs. Here, **The Ram Inn** (*raminn.co.uk*) is an attractive flint and brick pub that's a darkly stylish foodie paradise with rooms, open fires, and creative top notch food.

ABOVE: Ciders at a local farm shop.

BELOW: The South Downs is just as good for walking as paddling.

East Sussex

19 River Cuckmere and the Cuckmere Inn

- 4.8km (3 miles)
- Country to sea, peaceful, pretty
- Tidal river
- Out and back
- No licence needed

Seen from above, the Cuckmere Meanders are shiny ribbons curling through the grassy green landscape of the Seven Sisters Country Park in the South Downs. At the tail end, these bends of the River Cuckmere offer a gentle, easy paddle to enjoy birdsong and views of sunny fields and a valley that was, half a century ago, a salt marsh. Some of the silt in the meanders dates back to between 4,000 and 1,200 BC.

Part of the valley is a nature reserve, and a Site of Special Scientific Interest. In winter, wildfowl and Canadian geese can be spotted, while in summer butterflies fill the air.

The bends are natural but were made even slower and gentler by a cut created in 1847 to take the main flow of the river, making them very sheltered and still, with barely any current. For beginner paddlers it's a great introduction, especially as the base of Buzz Active, a not-for-profit watersports organisation run by East Sussex County Council, is right here, just inside the South Downs National

BELOW: Kayakers on the Cuckmere River's Cuckmere Meanders (photo: Buzz Active).

Park, next to the public car park, offering rental and trips. Independent paddlers must launch from the dedicated wharf in the South Car Park.

Buzz's three-hour there-and-back tour along this end section of the river is perfect, and there's a pub to pop to nearby afterwards. Its longer excursions run all the way up to Alfriston, a gorgeous village with very special pubs.

I took the shorter trip with a group of friends to celebrate a birthday, led by cheerful instructors Ollie and Connor and putting in via Buzz Active's slipway. As we chatted and bobbed along, low, vivid green hills rose on either side, and the shallows of the chalky beds were full of life. After an hour or so on the meanders, you pull in and get out to portage along a sandy path over a grassy bank to get onto

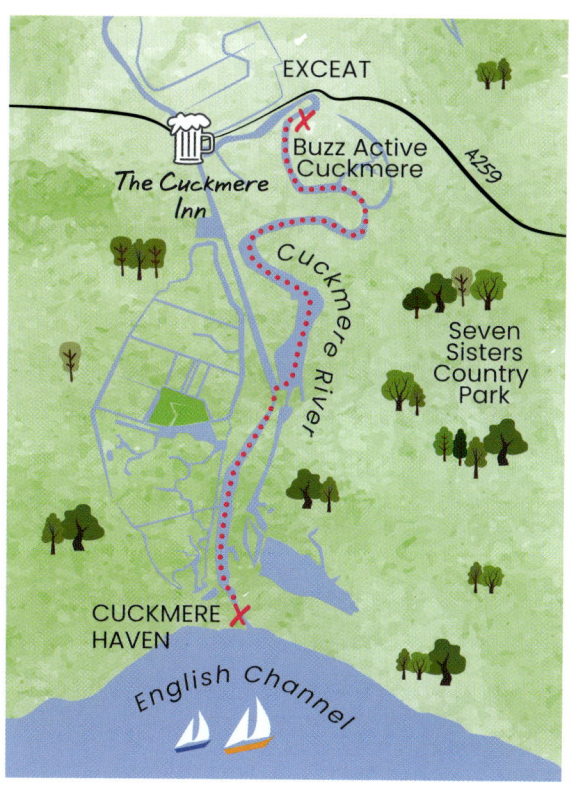

the canal cut (a straight, manmade section that cuts off the meanders as a faster route), for the final furlong along the tidal river to the sea.

Close to the sea, before the pebble beach, pull in on the sandy right bank and leave kayaks or SUPs there while you explore. The beach, with its views of the sheer white cliffs of the Seven Sisters, is lovely for a swim, and a dramatic hiking path runs over the cliff tops.

Above the beach are memorials to a tragedy of the Second World War, when a whole platoon of Canadian paratroopers, estimated to have been in their thousands, were killed in 1940 when they decided to camp here for a night. The area had been used for navigation by Nazi bombers. It was sometimes lit up as a decoy to divert them from Newhaven, and when Brighton was bombed any remaining explosives were dropped here. Despite locals warning them not to camp there, the soldiers' commanding officers didn't listen, and all sadly perished.

You can also see the remains of a 1930s miniature railway that

CLOCKWISE FROM TOP LEFT: Kayakers on the Cuckmere; the white cliffs of the Seven Sisters (photo: Buzz Active); a heron in the Cuckmere in the South Down; the Cuckmere Inn pub.

used to carry people to the river to row from Drusilla's Park (*drusillas.co.uk*), originally a popular tea room, now a zoo with rides.

After paddling back to the Buzz Active base (or car park if you're not on a tour), you need only walk a few minutes up the road to **The Cuckmere Inn**, a smart modern venue with views of the water beside Exceat Bridge. Harvey's Sussex Best is on tap, and out the back there's an expansive beer garden looking down on the river and up to the Downs. It's a lovely spot for a cocktail or a cuppa in the sun. Skewers, burgers, pizzas and pubby mains are on the menu. Another fantastic pub lies a ten-minute drive or an hour's walk over the hills: **The Tiger Inn**, the village green of East Dean, gorgeously low-ceilinged and quaint.

▶ Details

Rent SUPs, kayaks and giant Kata Kanu kayaks, and book guided trips with Buzz Active (*buzzactive.org.uk/locations/buzz-cuckmere*). Independent paddlers can use the dedicated wharf in the South Car Park (*sevensisters.org.uk/things-to-do/kayaking-paddle-boarding*). For more information, see (*gopaddling.info/rivers/river-cuckmere*). For pubs, see (*beachyhead.org.uk/the-tiger-inn*), and search for The Cuckmere Inn at (*vintageinn.co.uk*).

▶ Make a weekend of it

In Alfriston, **The Star** (*thepolizzicollection.com/the-star*) boutique hotel inhabits a revamped 15th-century inn with a beamed frontage. It's owned by interiors maestros Olga and Alex Polizzi. East Dean's Tiger Inn has pretty cream bedrooms.

▶ Alternative routes

When tides allow, it's possible to do a longer route along the Cuckmere River from near the source to sea, starting near Drusilla's Park and taking in Alfriston on the way downriver. Buzz Active also sells this as a five-hour guided trip twice a month (when there are the high spring and neap tides, when tides are much higher at the full and new moons). It starts from its base, going up to Alfriston for a lunch – often at the 14th-century pub, **The George** (*thegeorgealfriston.com*) – and back, in view of the White Horse carved in chalk on the hillside.

BELOW: The Littlington White Horse, carved into the chalky downs.

Kent

20 River Stour: Fordwich to Grove Ferry

- 7.5km (4.7 miles)
- Wildlife, rural, tranquil
- River
- One way
- No licence needed

Beavers had been hunted to near extinction for their pelts in the UK by the 16th century, but they are now so well re-established that there are thought to be some 140 individuals living on a stretch near the small city of Canterbury.

The most enchanting way to learn more about these furry fellows, and to see them for yourself in the wild, is with a sunset safari by kayak or paddleboard on the chalkstream waterway, which handily ends at a riverside pub.

It's absolutely possible to paddle here with your own kit; there's a public car park at Grove Ferry next to the pub's one, with nearby water access, but I'd really recommend Canoe Wild. As well as hiring out kit, this operation offers an atmospheric guided tour in the warmer months, which, as long as you listen to the guides' advice and keep quiet, will increase your chance of seeing nature's cutest carpenters in the wild. The guides will help you time your paddle so you're passing the spots the beavers visit most frequently at dusk, when they're most active. Some extended trips also include a talk about the beavers.

BELOW: Beavers are most active at dusk on the River Stour.

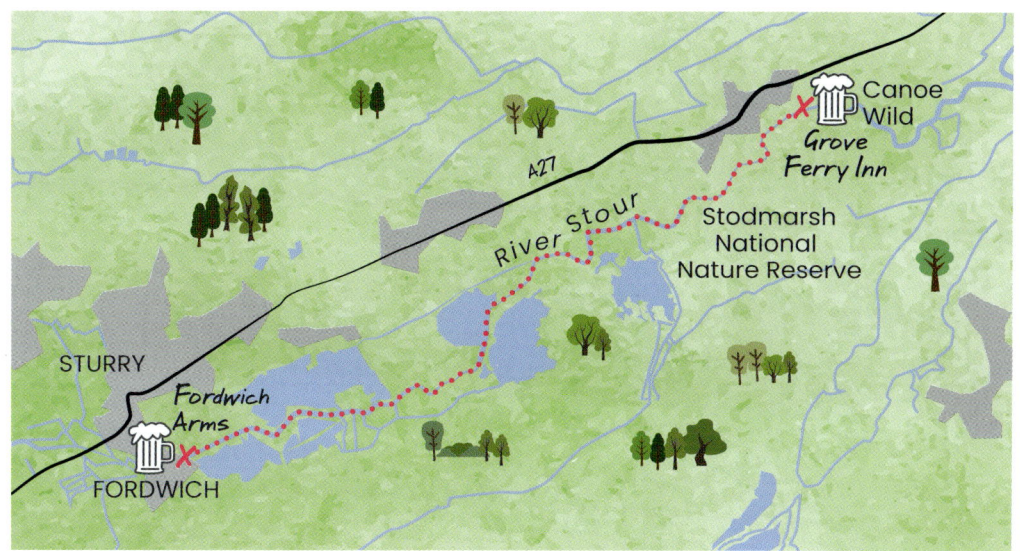

I joined one in early September, parking at Grove Ferry to be whisked by minibus to the start point at the village of Fordwich, enabling a one-way route. An amazing foodie pub, the **Fordwich Arms**, is near the start, a fine dining establishment with tasting menus featuring dishes such as Scottish langoustine with gooseberry. It would be well worth coming early for a special lunch before the paddle. A lovely terrace has tables outside overlooking the water.

Lovely red and green Canadian-style canoes were lined up at the start point by the narrow stream of Evian-clear water, through which green fronds trailed like mermaids' hair. Fish skittered and the late evening sun danced across the surface.

As we set out, we were told that – obviously – staying quiet is the key. 'If you do see one,' said guides Tom Crowther and Ollie Andrews, 'don't shout out, "I've seen a beaver!" just quietly put your paddle in the air to indicate to others.' Easier said than done for such an exciting spot. On the evening of my departure the tour was at maximum capacity (six boats), and not everyone had got the memo about keeping schtum. But we soon spread out and my friend and co-paddler Nell and I managed to drift away from the noisy ones, to find some peace.

The narrow river's tree-lined banks sometimes gave way to fields rising over small hills like patchwork quilts, and when we came to Bootleg Lake, the sky exploded into golden pink, giving us

BELOW: Paddling a Canadian-style canoe is a great way to approach wildlife silently.

RIGHT: Fairy lights outside the Grover Ferry Arms.

BELOW: Sundown at Bootleg Lake.

no choice but to linger and soak up the silent sunset scene. Around the edges of the lake, many beavers have their dens, one local paddler told me, and people often walk down here to see them.

Beavers were reintroduced at Ham Fen, a Kent Wildlife Reserve (*kentwildlifetrust.org.uk*) near Sandwich, at the sea-end of the Stour in 2000. As the last remaining area of fenland in Kent, it was the perfect territory and the beavers thrived. The project led the way for other projects throughout the country. Beavers are 'ecosystem engineers', who improve wetland areas by coppicing vegetation and reducing flooding, a task made evermore important as the climate crisis ramps up.

As the river passed beside Stodmarsh National Nature Reserve, we began to notice mudslides pocked with pawprints: the slippery chutes where the animals enter the water.

We didn't spot them here, alas (probably too much chatting). But then, suddenly, two loud splashes – and something sizeable careered into the water. 'Definitely a beaver,' whispered the guides. Then, as it started to get properly dark, they pointed towards the banks. A dark shadowy shape was moving under some branches on the muddy left bank. Another loud splosh. 'When they hear something coming, beavers whack their wide tails onto the water, to scare away predators,' said the guides. The sound was definitely that. We might not have got the classic beaver money shot, seeing one swimming with a big log between its teeth, but even a shadowy splosh felt Attenborough-level exciting, especially on a humid night under a blazing Milky Way.

The finale of the route is a fairy-lit return alongside the pub garden, passing under a bridge lit up with dangling lights that lends the feel of a fairground boat ride.

Pulling in at a jetty and hauling the canoes onto the bank, I looked up at a magnificent starry sky, the perfect end to a Kentish safari. And there we were at **The Grove Ferry Inn**. The ivy-wreathed Shepherd Neame pub may have dated decor and a few too many big dogs in the bar for my liking, but there's often live music, and the huge riverside terrace is a great place to relax with a drink. We waved off the group and assured the guides we'd had a great time though we weren't so lucky with the spotting. 'I've seen as many as 14 beavers in one night before,' one confided. Just remember to keep quiet and you may too.

▶ Details

Canoe Wild (*canoewild.co.uk/wildlife-sunset-tour*) offers SUP, canoe and kayak hire, and tours including transport for one-way trips, from its base in Fordwich. See Paddle UK's web page (*gopaddling.info/rivers/river-stour-in-kent*) for information. The pub is (*www.groveferryinn.co.uk*).

▶ Make a weekend of it

The Grove Ferry Inn has elegant bedrooms; the Fordwich Arms (*fordwicharms.co.uk*) has a holiday cottage. South of Canterbury, The Pig At Bridge Place (*thepighotel.com*) is a fabulous boutique option.

BELOW: Canoe Wild's evening beaver safari is a wonderful, slow-paced and peaceful paddle, ending at a pub.

The East

Suffolk/Essex

21 Stour Valley: Sudbury to Bures

- 9.7km (6 miles)
- Rural, peaceful, beauty
- River
- One way
- Licence needed

The beautiful Stour Valley, following the border of Suffolk and Essex, is one of those 'secret' corners of Britain, as travel writers like to say. Obviously there's no such thing really, but it's true that this part of East Anglia is relatively overlooked, aside from a few famous pockets associated with the artist John Constable. His works depict spots such as Flatford, the setting for his most famous painting, *The Hay Wain*, and *The Vale of Dedham*.

This 76 km (47 mile) long river flows from east Cambridgeshire to the North Sea and has an olde worlde feeling, Its quieter, lesser-known stretches are idyllic for a day's paddle, or even a multi-day adventure with stops at campsites or country hotels along the way. It's a calm, pretty river particularly well-suited to that kind of trip.

This route starts in Sudbury and winds downriver to Bures. It's a calm, leafy three-hour glide passing under willow trees and places where the river slows to form deep, velvety pools that are perfect for swimming. You'll see few other people, and stop off at several heartwarmingly old-school pubs along the way. Handily there's a railway station at both ends too; handy for independent paddlers leaving a car at one end.

I went on a Canadian canoe excursion with local operator Elemental Outdoors, meeting in Sudbury, an attractive Suffolk town built on the wool industry. Today it's peppered with sunny-yellow buildings and posh shops. The put-in is the public slipway

BELOW: Sections of the River Stour are very narrow and bristling with vegetation.

at Katherine's Quay by The Granary on Quay Lane. You can buy a day's licence at the office of the River Stour Trust if you don't have an annual pass and are going independently. There is a car park and tea room.

The river is narrow and tranquil here. Reeds are fronded and mottled with pond weed, and overhung by trees whose glossy, green reflections are painted across the water surface. Bunting was strung above the river when we set out in July, bringing a festive atmosphere to our jolly summer's outing. Sudbury Rowing Club soon comes up, before a portage around Great Cornard lock.

As the river opens out, soon you're at the first stop, **The Henny Swan**, with a lovely big lawned beer garden down to the water. Inside the dark wood-panelled interior you'll find Lacons Norfolk Gem best bitter on tap, along with Juvel and Adnams Ghost Ship, and simple pub grub. Paddlers are welcome to arrive by water, but can only make their initial launch from here if they buy a pass in the pub, and park elsewhere. There's a SUP hire place here too.

Off we went again, down a tight emerald channel that could be a tributary of the Amazon, and then we floated slowly under the dangling fringes of willow trees – as if riding one of those early 20th-century tunnel of love fairground rides. There's a lovely swim spot coming up, ringed in by lush greenery, where we shared a picnic and enjoyed a dip.

A little excitement next at the rushy drop of Shalford weir; some paddle over it but you should really portage. Then there are views of butter yellow fields in the distance as the river curves close to a railway line. Pull onto the right bank, cross the train track very carefully and a few minutes' walk brings you to **The Lamarsh Lion**, a pleasingly small and simple Essex community pub, dating to the 14th century.

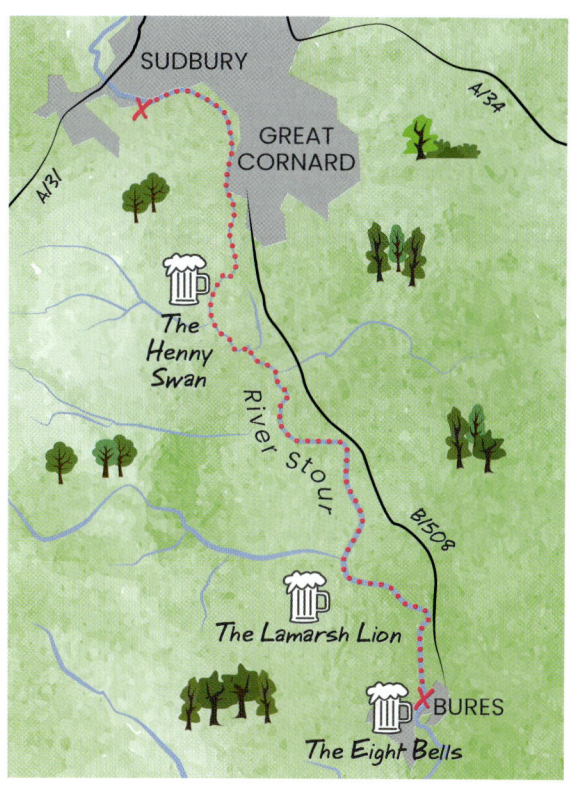

BELOW: The terrace of the Henny Swan pub.

CLOCKWISE FROM TOP LEFT: Stour Valley gold on tap at the Eight Bells in Bures; weeping willows line the banks; paddleboarders near the Henny Swan; the granary at Sudbury.

Back on the river, the next and final stop is Bures, a lovely village of timber-framed houses dating to the 14th–16th centuries, which spans the Suffolk-Essex border. At the back of the riverside common, where locals often play quoits, is the charming **Eight Bells**, a CAMRA pub surrounded by pink hollyhocks. Try the Stour Valley Gold from Nethergate, Greene King's Abbot Ale, a lemon and ginger tinged New Tricks golden ale, or good old Timothy Taylor's Landlord. The decor is a blast from the past – horse brasses alongside old black and white photos.

If you have time, walk to St Stephen's chapel, built in 1220, behind which is a white dragon carved into the hillside, commemorating a dragon that arrived in Bures in 1405. The tale isn't so tall as it might sound. There was, apparently, a crocodile brought back from the Crusades to the Tower of London, which escaped and made its way into the Essex marshes and eventually the Stour. Keep a wary eye out for descendants as you paddle.

▶ Details

Hire canoes, kayaks and paddleboards, or arrange guided paddling trips on the River Stour, including multi-day journeys involving overnight camping, with Elemental Outdoors (*elemental-outdoors.com/elemental-adventures*). It also arranges cycling, hiking and swimming trips. Buy licences at (*riversourtrust.org*). For the pubs, see (*thehennyswan.co.uk*), (*lamarshlion.co.uk*) and for the Eight Bells (*suffolk.camra.org.uk/pub/1264*).

▶ Make a weekend of it

In Sudbury, try The Mill Hotel (*suryahotels.co.uk/themillhotel*), in a converted watermill, with meadow views and a sunny terrace.

▶ Alternative routes

A longer 42km (26 mile) route follows the same way from Sudbury but continues east to Cattawade. The first stage, Sudbury to Nayland is a six- to seven-hour paddle; the Eight Bells in Bures makes a good halfway stop. There's a campsite by the river in Nayland, called Rushbanks Farm (*rushbankscampsite.co.uk*), which offers canoe hire. Nayland to Cattawade is another six hours, passing through Stratford St Mary, Dedham and Flatford. In Dedham, the gorgeous, yolk-coloured Sun Inn (*thesuninndedham.com*) is a five-minute walk from the river.

ABOVE: Load up a Canadian canoe for a leisurely day on the River Stour.

Cambridgeshire

22 River Cam: Cambridge to Grantchester

- 16km (10 miles)
- City, culture, history
- River
- Out and back
- Licence needed

Could there be a more beautiful city to paddle through than Cambridge, with its spires and riverside college grounds, historic buildings and bridges?

Being punted gently along the Cam by a superiorly educated student is, of course, de rigueur to see this beautiful city's finest sights: the intricate masonry of the famous bridges, the soaring colleges… the hammered undergrads lolling on the grass.

But while no commercial kayak or SUP tours are currently allowed to go through the centre, those with their own kit can paddle themselves – as long as they display their British waterways licence number on the side of their vessel. This opens a world of wonder, a world-famous stretch of river that feels like

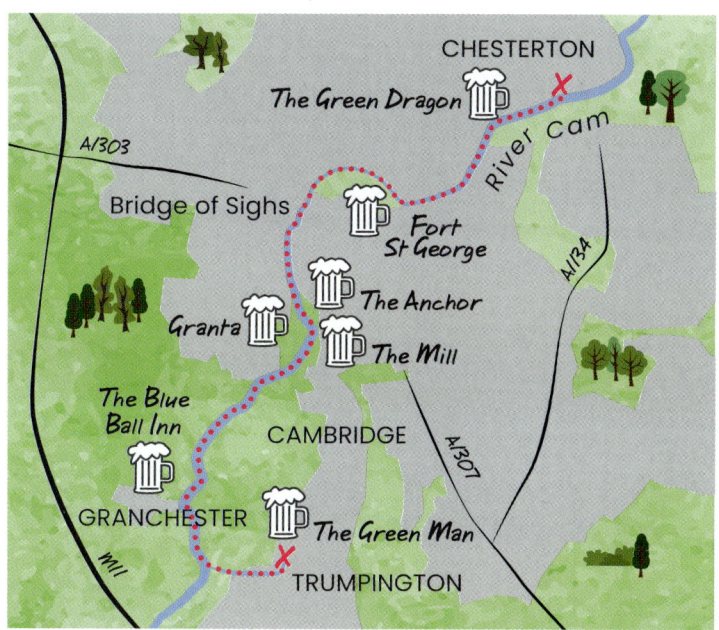

floating through a museum. Paddlers can enjoy the ultimate perspective on the gorgeous grassy grounds of Jesus College, the Backs and the Bridge of Sighs, without paying the exorbitant price for being poled along in a punt.

The following route could be adapted to be shorter, but you might find you're having so much fun you go way farther than expected. Starting in the green north of the city, it takes in parks, rowing clubs, the historic centre and then green swathes and wild swimming spots to the south, all the way out to the gorgeous village of Grantchester, where Lord Byron famously dipped. Spend a day exploring this route and you'll feel like you've had a full holiday; a cultural break, nature immersion and wellbeing retreat all in one. And the pubs? Only some of the most culturally important in the land.

Scudamores, the city's punting company, hires out kayaks near the main colleges, but you're only allowed to use them to go south out of the city to Grantchester.

So where to start? Many of the residential streets to the north of the city, between Cambridge North railway station and the River Cam, are free to park on, and there's a tiny riverside car park at Chesterton. There's easy access to the water around Abbey Chesterton Bridge from the immaculate cycling and walking

OPPOSITE: Canoes for rent at the Granta pub.

BELOW: Paddling south out of the city to Grantchester.

22 RIVER CAM 113

CLOCKWISE FROM TOP LEFT: Benches outside the Fort St George pub; the Cam is lined with pubs, cafes, and boats for hire; Trinity College as seen while paddleboarding past; a terrace of the Granta pub overlooks the water.

paths that run alongside. I opted for that.

Heading south, with Stourbridge Common on the south bank, you'll pass **The Green Dragon** on the north side, whose willow-draped beer garden runs down to the water, next to a slipway covered in duck poo. Thought to be the city's oldest coaching house and built in the 16th century, it's where JRR Tolkien found inspiration for *The Hobbit* and *The Lord of The Rings*, and where Oliver Cromwell supposedly sat with friends practising knife-throwing into the fire lintel. If you're paddling this route as an out and back, this is the pub to end on.

On a hot September day I enjoyed this slow, languorous paddle, nosing at waterside gardens with their pizza ovens and swings, private jetties and luxury office sheds, wondering if the person typing inside was a uni professor or a famous author.

LEFT: Jesus College can be admired from the water.

Cambridge inspires the imagination. Along the Cam you'll pass college rowing clubs, cyclists, walkers, troupes of tourists, even fishermen settled in for the day, as well as the grassy commons where cattle have grazed for centuries. Watch out for the rowers and stick to the right as they pelt along. There are a few not-so-pretty bits as you come into town but that's a fleeting precursor to the architectural wonders soon to come.

Fort Saint George with a beer garden on Midsummer Common and riverside benches, is next, and another of the oldest pubs on the Cam, built in the 16th century. Inside, oars decorate the walls. It makes a lovely stop for a cup of tea, or for an early lunch.

Passing Jesus Green, you're entering punt territory, and you'll have to jostle along with the well-spoken tour guides charging past with their 5m (16ft) poles. The air becomes thick with snippets of 'Henry VIII' this and 'King John' that. Even if you don't mean to piggyback on the historic tours the tourists have paid good money for, you can't help but garner all sorts of historical low down for free as you follow in their wake. Look out for the **Pimms Punt**, a floating bar dispensing the classic English summer drink and beer. But the showstoppers are up next: the incredibly intricate Bridge of Sighs at St John's College, covered and with an arched base like its Venetian namesake; the Backs university fields; Queens' College's quirky wooden footbridge; the Mathematical Bridge.

Then you're into one of the most fun and bustling parts of the river, the Mill Pond, which is lined with pubs. **The Anchor** on the east side supplies a steady stream of pints to students sitting on the grass and terrace. Adjacent is the **Granta** pub on a little side cut, with a lovely covered balcony over the water. Another option is

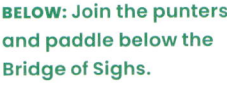

BELOW: Join the punters and paddle below the Bridge of Sighs.

116 THE EAST

CAMRA award winner **The Mill**, where you can take drinks out to the Mill Pond. The city's punt company, Scudamores is here.

You could turn around here, and you would have had a brilliant day, but you may well feel the urge for somewhere more verdant and peaceful, so follow the main flow of the river out into calm, quiet countryside, where trees shade the water. Pass the private grounds of the Newnham Riverbank Club (nrclub.org), for wild swimmers, and if you feel like it join others taking a tranquil dip a little further on beside Grantchester Meadows, about 6.4km (4 miles) from your start.

The Lammas Land car park here is a handy place to leave a vehicle if you're doing a two-car shuffle. But carry on, and a little further upriver is the beautiful village of Grantchester, in whose meadows the Bloomsbury set languished over picnics. The **Blue Ball Inn** is an appealing stop here, or close by, the neighbouring village of Trumpington has several more gorgeous pubs, including the 400-year old **Green Man** with a riverside beer garden. Grantchester has car parks and river access, including at Byron's Pool, where the writer famously swam, now a nature reserve. The paddle all the way to Grantchester is 8km (5 miles), so it's a hefty 16km (10 miles) there and back. But completing this myself I found it one of the most delightful paddles of the book.

BELOW: It's great fun to paddle through the city.

▶ Details

For the pubs, see (greendragoncambridge.co.uk), (greeneking.co.uk/pubs/cambridgeshire/fort-st-george), (instagram.com/pimmspunt), (anchorcambridge.com), (greeneking.co.uk /pubs/cambridgeshire/granta), (themillpubcambridge.com), (blueballgrantchester.co.uk), (thegrantchestergreenman.com). See Paddle UK's web page for parking and getting in points (gopaddling.info/rivers/river-cam). Scudamores (scudamores.com/grantchester-kayak-hire) hires kayaks for paddles to Grantchester. Display your licence number on your vessel.

▶ Make a weekend of it

In the city, The Varsity (thevarsityhotel.co.uk) boutique hotel has a very fun rooftop terrace for cocktails, cool, colourful rooms and a small spa with an indoor hot tub looking out to the river. In Grantchester, The Blue Ball Inn and Lord Byron Inn B&B (lordbyroninn.co.uk) have rooms.

Norfolk

23 Norfolk Rivers and Broads: River Waveney

—	8.4km (5.2 miles)
⊙	Peaceful, green, nature
～	River
=	Out and back
▪	Licence needed

With their wide peaceful lakes linked by pretty rivers, their salty proximity to the sea and bewitching villages, the Norfolk Broads are a paradise for paddlers.

It's here that The Canoe Man was one of the originators of the UK's paddle trip industry as it is known today, launching gentle, expert-led, knowledge-imparting tours back in the Noughties, and inspiring copycats up and down the country.

Today, The Canoe Man has expanded his remit and expertise to offer paddle trips that involve bushcraft classes, otter spotting and foraging on his brilliant and varied menu. Many of these take in the unflashy pubs of the Norfolk Broads and its rivers. There are overnight trips to camp out in bivvy bags (or tents for the wusses) on the company's own patch of land, Wild Wood, as well as one-way journeys of several hours down the rivers Bure, Yare and Waveney, or simple hire of kayaks, SUPs and canoes from four bases in the area.

One of the most peaceful options is a paddle up to the un-navigable (for boats), and hence far less busy, stretches of the River Waveney, an out-and-back which happens to take in an

BELOW: The town of Beccles (photo: iStock).

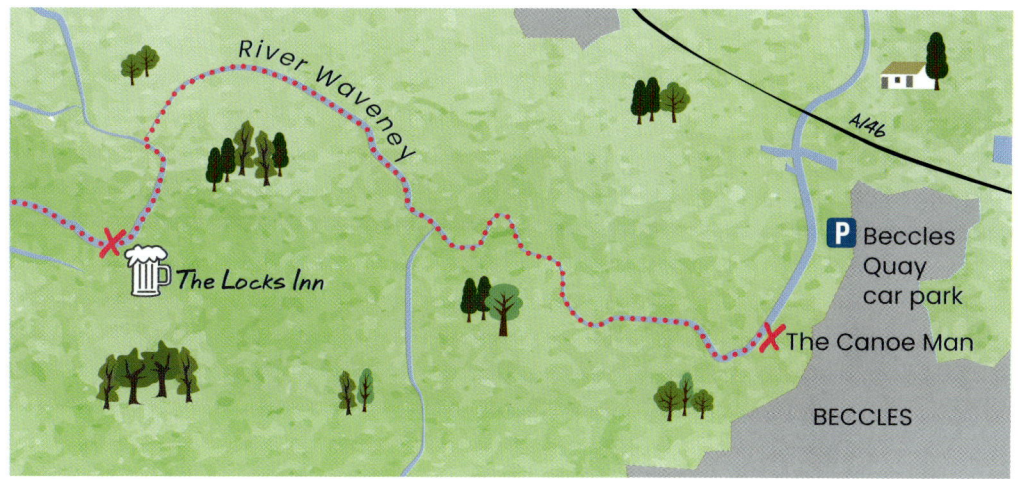

excellent pub with an uplifting tale behind it.

From the pretty market town of Beccles (actually in Suffolk; you're on the border here), you'll head upstream west along the narrow, green and wiggly River Waveney.

The Canoe Man's hire place is at Beccles's Lido, so perfect your day even more by starting or finishing with a swim in one of Norfolk's few outdoor pools. Then you're off on a voyage of relaxation and discovery through a green and pleasant land. After about an hour and a half, you'll reach the pub pitstop on the Norfolk/Suffolk border, which has a floating pontoon to welcome paddlers. A few years ago, in 2020, **The Locks Inn** was suddenly put up for auction and looked like it might be a goner, but the local community stepped in, bought it, and it's been run as a community venue since. It now has the widest ownership in the country, say its 1,600 shareholders. Local ales, live music, pub grub and a grassy, riverside garden full of benches make it a favourite.

Don't get too carried away, though, as you'll want to paddle on a little way further upstream to enjoy the tranquillity of the upper section, going as far as you like before turning about for the easy float downstream back to the start (and that swim).

▸ Details

Arrange hire from Norwich, Beccles, Coltishall or Wroxham, or one- or two-way trips, including overnight adventures, with The Canoe Man (*thecanoeman.com*). For the pub, see (*thelocksinn.com*).

CLOCKWISE FROM RIGHT:
A swan on the River Bure; a peaceful morning on the Norfolk Broads; the River Waveney at Geldeston; Coltishall (all photos: iStock).

ABOVE: Trees and fields line the banks of the River Waveney (photo: iStock).

Independent paddlers can park at Beccles Quay Car Park by the water. Beccles Yacht Station has a slipway to launch from, but check with the harbourmaster as there may be a charge. There's also a cafe. The Big Dog Ferry (*bigdogferry.co.uk*) is a small boat service running between Beccles and the Locks Inn. For information about paddling the River Waveney, see (*gopaddling.info/rivers/river-waveney*), and for the Norfolk Broads, see the regional websites (*broads-authority.gov.uk/boating/navigating-the-broads/canoeing,-kayaking-and-paddleboarding*) and (*visitthebroads.co.uk/things-to-do/sports/canoekayakpadboard*).

▶ Make a weekend of it

Near the Locks Inn, on the outskirts of Geldeston, Three Rivers Pitch and Paddle (*threeriverscamping.co.uk*) has camping pitches right on the riverbanks, or try the smart riverside Waveney House Hotel (*waveneyhousehotel.co.uk*) in Beccles. The Locks Inn lists local accommodation, from campsites to AirBnBs, on its website (*thelocksinn.com/accommodation*).

▶ Alternative route

Another brilliant Canoe Man option along the River Bure starts out with a ride aboard the Bure Valley Steam Railway (*bvrw.co.uk*) from Wroxham to Buxton, where you walk ten minutes to the launch point on the river, paddling with the flow back down to Wroxham. The first section is non-navigable so free of other boats until Coltishall, called the gateway to the Broads, where you can stop at the waterside **Rising Sun** (*risingsuncoltishall.co.uk*) pub on the way. It does wood-fired pizzas. This adventure takes around five hours in all.

What else would this trip be called, but 'the paddle steamer' (*thecanoeman.com/bure-valley-paddle-steamer*).

Norfolk

24 Norfolk Rivers and Broads: Norwich and River Wensum

- 10.5km (6.5 miles)
- Urban, rural, pub crawl
- River
- One way
- Licence needed

The Norfolk Broads are blessed with endless kayaking and paddleboarding opportunities across their network of 30 shallow lakes, interlinked with 320km (200 miles) of waterways and wetlands. One of the less obvious, but no less spectacular, routes leads out from the centre of Norwich along the River Wensum, providing an easy access no-brainer paddle.

While following a major route rather than exploring the quieter, wildlife-filled lakes the Broads National Park is famed for, it nevertheless gives a taste of what boating here is all about, with one or two mini-Broads encircled by high rushes at the end. An advantage is the easy accessibility of a city departure point, especially if coming by train, but it has the even greater benefit

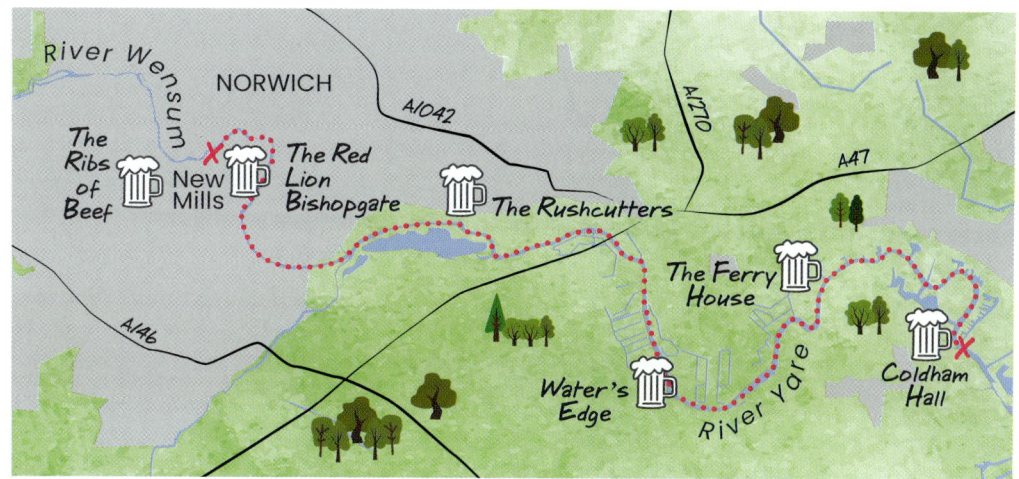

of stringing together several characterful riverside pubs.

How could I not include a tour with a company whose name is Pub and Paddle? That's the moniker of this friendly and professional outfit based in Norwich, a city that was once a byword for middle-of-the-road, Partridge-endorsed mediocrity, but has in recent years become thoroughly cool. While going with this canoe company is a pleasure, not least because its founder, Nick Hanington, builds his own wooden boats, it is of course possible to go the route independently. Put in at New Mills in the centre, near Westwick Street car park.

Local man Nick has offered canoe and kayak hire here since 2015, with various routes available, from a two-hour city centre paddle to a seven-hour day following the Wensum south-east from the city as it flows towards and into the River Yare, via six or more pubs. Needless to say, you should not be boozing at every one. Paddling under the influence is a bad idea, and Nick is determined to make this clear, adamant this trip isn't an opportunity for a waterborne smash-up. Customers who arrive with clinking bags will be turned away – one guy who arrived with a whole tray of Jägermeister shots was sent packing. 'What we're offering is a canoe experience with some pubs, not some kind of bar crawl,' he says. Enjoying the pubs for a cuppa, a snack, lunch and a pint at the very end is the best way.

All these self-led tours depart from Pub and Paddle's dedicated wooden jetty right beside the **Ribs of Beef**, a lively real ale pub with a small nook of a stone terrace over the river and

OPPOSITE: The Rushcutters pub in Thorpe St Andrew.

BELOW: Tables at the Ribs of Beef overlook the River Wensum in Norwich.

CLOCKWISE FROM TOP LEFT: Pub and Paddle offers a brilliant day out on the River Wensum; starting out from Norwich; the river soon opens up and quietens down as you head east out of the city.

LEFT: The outside of the Ribs of Beef by the riverside.

tables nudging onto Fye bridge. A few sections remain of the original 14th-century pub building, largely destroyed in the city's Great Fire of 1507. Its interior features a French pewter bar.

I opted for the longest route, for which Nick allows seven hours, though I completed it in five because I was alone so didn't spend ages bantering in the pubs. The shorter routes turn back at various points along the way, but on this one you leave the canoes at the end, returning by cab. Norwich is only 32km (20 miles) up the tidal Yare from the sea at Great Yarmouth, so it's best to set out around high tide, carried by the outgoing tide.

Coming through the city under Fye bridge, you pass gardens and, on the right, Cow Tower, a defensive artillery blockhouse dating to 1398. You'll pass the **Red Lion Bishopgate** on the right, which offers paddleboard hire and lessons. Weaving through the town's hotch-potch of dilapidated sheds, gardens, commercial businesses and pretty willow trees, you'll come out past Norwich Canoe Club and join the River Yare to meander into the countryside.

Where the river divides, take the cut on the left passing Thorpe-St-Andrew, where the simple **Rivergarden** pub has benches along the left bank. Soon after, **The Rushcutters Arms** is a lovely 16th-century waterside pub, frequented as much by cyclists and walkers following the Wherryman's Way as by boaters. This affluent village has been described as 'the Richmond

ABOVE: The final stop at the Coldham Hall pub.

of Norwich' and is a lovely place to pause for lunch (pork and cider terrine, perhaps, baked camembert, pies or steaks). Shorter trips turn back here. To the south is Whitlingham Great Broad, if you have time to explore further.

Passing Thorpe Ferry Cafe on the left, and a couple of marinas, paddle under the A47 then appreciate that you're at last entering peaceful idyllic countryside, droned by blue dragonflies and kingfishers. Another wonderful option, the 17th-century **Water's Edge** soon follows on a wide stretch of river. It took me 45 minutes to get here from Thorpe-St-Andrew. There's loads of space to pull in, tons of outdoor seating on a sleek deck, as well as a cosy firelit interior and a menu offering mussels and local ales.

After another 45 minutes or so of green-fronded loveliness, the **Surlingham Ferry House** is a community-spirited boaters' tavern barely changed since it was founded in 1725. A friendly atmosphere prevails, helped by Adnams ales on tap and a disco ball. You've made it 10.5km (6.5 miles) downriver from Norwich.

After the village of Brundall Gardens, channels lead off into small Broads, such as Bargate on the south side, hemmed in by high reeds. Pause to float and tune in to the peeps and clicks of birds, plopping fish and bubbles rising from the depths. Then your final destination, **Coldham Hall** provides a last quaint stop for pub grub and drinks – including wine from the village's Winbirri vineyard (*winbirri.com*) – on its huge waterside deck. When you're done, get a taxi back to the start (Nick collects the canoes here).

▶ Details

Pub and Paddle (*pubandpaddle.com*) offers tours and canoe hire with route maps. For information on exploring the area, see (*broads-authority.gov.uk*), (*norfolkbroads.com*) and (*gopaddling.info/rivers/river-wensum*). For the pubs, see (*ribsofbeef.co.uk*), (*redlionbishopgate.co.uk*), (*therivergardennorwich.com*), (*chefandbrewer.com/pubs/norfolk/rushcutters-arms*), (*watersedgewoodsend.co.uk*), (*surlinghamferry.co.uk*) and (*coldhamhall.com*).

▶ Make a weekend of it

Stay in Norwich's Assembly House (*assemblyhousenorwich.co.uk*), whose 15 bedrooms have four-poster beds and 'secret garden' terraces.

The Midlands

Warwickshire

25 Rivers Avon and Leam: Warwick to Leamington Spa

—	6.4 to 12.9km (4 to 8 miles)
◉	History, peace, urban
〜	River
=	One way or out and back
▪	Licence needed

Dating back 1,100 years, Warwick Castle is one of Britain's most important and best-preserved buildings. Like many of the world's great castles, it was built in an advantageous position above a wide, powerful river – in this case, the River Avon – to aid trade and protect it from attack. Its high stone walls, battlements, and turreted towers are an imposing sight from any perspective, but especially so from the water.

These days it's most likely school children and theme park passholders who will be gazing down from the slitted windows from which medieval archers once aimed. The company Merlin owns the spectacular castle and has added everything from a maze and bird of prey displays to glamping. But paddling up to it erases all that from sight, so you can witness the towering fortress just as its assailants did centuries ago. Away from the tourist throngs, you can take your time looking at the exterior alone for the best sort of sightseeing.

On this relaxed paddle from Warwick, heading west to Royal Leamington Spa, the castle is your dramatic start for a peaceful tour between two interesting, historic towns. A luscious deep green stretch of wide water links the two Midlands towns, with little

BELOW: Warwick Castle looks grand and imposing from the water.

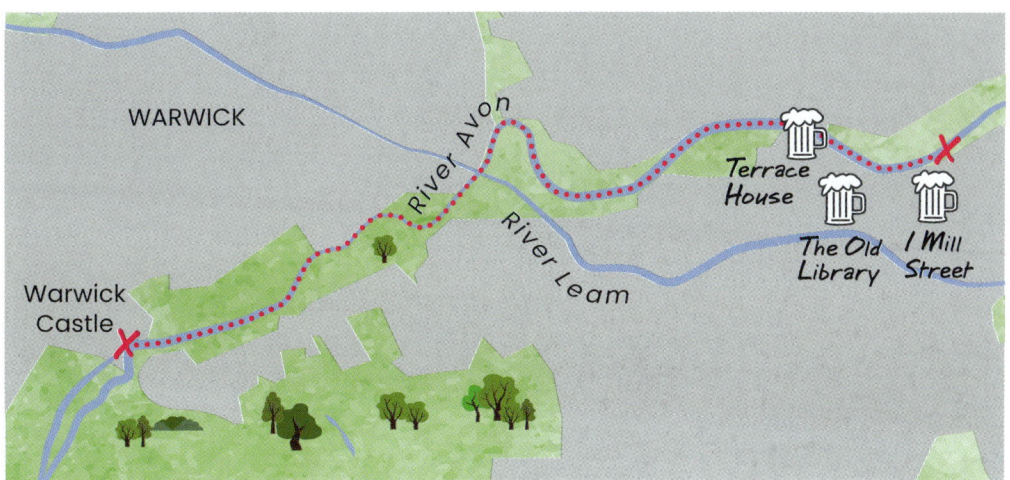

evidence of urban development along the riverbanks, and only geese and the occasional rower passing by. Both have kayak/SUP hire places, so it's easy to do a there-and-back in either direction. Leamington has a waterside bar so I opted to paddle from Warwick, then deflated and rolled my own SUP in Leamington, returning by taxi.

Starting off from Warwick, after about a kilometre and a half (one mile) you'll turn right (east) onto the River Leam. The surroundings here become a little more developed, but there are still lilypads and fields. Portage up the stepped stone levels at Princess Drive Weir, and carry on. You'll reach Victoria Park on the south bank and the lovely Jephson Gardens, a typical Victorian park, then arrive into a pond full of geese, swans and ducks, under Mill Bridge Weir and the grand blue Victorian suspension bridge, Mill Bridge. Exit on the south side, up an alley to Mill Road.

Your first port of call might be **1 Mill Street** (weekdays only) a cool, red-brick co-working space, which operates an open-to-all coffeeshop and a bar serving its own pilsner.

Leam Boat Centre is right here too. Their friendly staff told me their favourite post-paddle pub is **The Old Library**, a couple of minutes' walk away on Bath Street. It has a bit of a sports pub vibe, but wood-panelled booths too, and a nice little beer garden looking onto All Saints church.

Classier is the riverside bar **The Terrace**, where an elegant covered colonnade (very Jane Austen visits the Midlands) overlooks the bit of the Leam you've just paddled. Inside, pastel-

BELOW: Heading east from the castle along the River Avon.

25 RIVERS AVON AND LEAM 129

CLOCKWISE FROM TOP LEFT: A tunnel on the River Avon; a quiet stretch by the castle; The Terrace bar has a covered colonnade overlooking the River Leam; The Old Library is a favourite with paddlers in Leamington Spa.

coloured rooms with high ceilings and chandeliers lend a Bridgerton vibe. Come for ciders and draught ales, Belgian beers such as super-strength Kwak, or a marsala chai. The menu ranges from herby scallops and lobster linguine to burgers and roasts.

▶ Details

For the pubs, see The Old Library (*greatukpubs.co.uk /old-library-leamington-spa*), (*theterrace.uk*), (*1millstreet.com/bar*). Almost next to the castle, Warwick Boats (*warwickboats.co.uk*) hires out kayaks, canoes and paddleboards and offers tuition. To really jar with the historic surroundings, they also offer dragon pedalos, pedal swans, and Chinese dragon boats. In Leamington, the well-established Leam Boat Centre (*leamboatcentre.com*), which dates to 1901, has kayaks, SUPS, trips and lessons. See Paddle UK's website (*gopaddling.info*). If you don't have an annual waterways licence, buy a short term one on the Avon Navigation Trust website (*avonnavigationtrust.org*). There are car parks at both ends, and a bus service and railway link the towns.

▶ Make a weekend of it

Stay in the attractive grounds of Warwick Castle (*warwick-castle.com*) among towering trees in the medieval-style Knight's Lodge cabins and glamping tents, metres from the water. With your own kit you could paddle a little way west on the shallow, narrow channel towards the castle before getting stuck at its high weir, or head east out along the Avon.

▶ Alternative route

The Avon runs north to south between Warwick and Leamington, dividing them. Paddle north and after five or six kilometres (three or four miles) you will find **The Saxon Mill** (*saxonmill.co.uk*), a gorgeous riverside pub. Sit on the terrace overlooking the water and order dishes such as rotisserie chicken or slow-cooked pork belly that surpass the usual pub fare.

Another option is to paddle the Grand Union canal on the southern side of Leamington Spa, where the **Micro Pug** bar (*themicropug.com*) has a secret door hidden in a Smeg fridge that leads to a retro-themed bar downstairs, with a garden by the canal path. Nearby, **The Moorings** pub (*themoorings.co.uk*) has funky interiors, live music and waterside seating.

26 Kinver and the Staffordshire and Worcester Canal

Staffordshire

- 3.2km (2 miles)
- Countryside, history, easy
- Canal
- Out and back
- Licence needed

They may be straight and flat, often requiring a there-and-back route, but canal paddles are the easiest and safest. This makes them ideal for beginners, or for a stress-free paddle and, as a bonus, they require no navigational skills. Not without their charms, then, yet few are as pretty as the Kinver stretch of the Staffordshire and Worcester canal, with its tall trees, grassy banks, interesting old bridges and tollhouses.

This is a waterway with a fascinating history – it was hugely important to the development of Great Britain itself. One of the major Midlands arteries, the canal facilitated trade with the world, in particular, the transportation of pottery from Stoke on Trent. Running for 74km (46 miles), the canal connects to the River Severn at one end, near Stourport, and the Stourport Basins, which link to Bristol and thus the sea.

Kinver village, near Stourbridge, is full of attractive half-timbered buildings, and the River Stour runs through it.

The pub you are heading to, **The Vine**, lies in Kinver itself, right beside the canal. It's a charming little one-room place with a large beer garden by the water. It has the feel of an old wooden church, with high gabled ceilings and pew-like benches, though it was converted from two cottages. The pub also happens to be the base of River Severn Canoes, which offers hire of sit-on-top kayaks at weekends and during school holidays. Hire lasts for 90 minutes, enough time to explore a couple of miles of this easy-going route

BELOW: Autumn colours on a Staffordshire riverbank (photo: iStock).

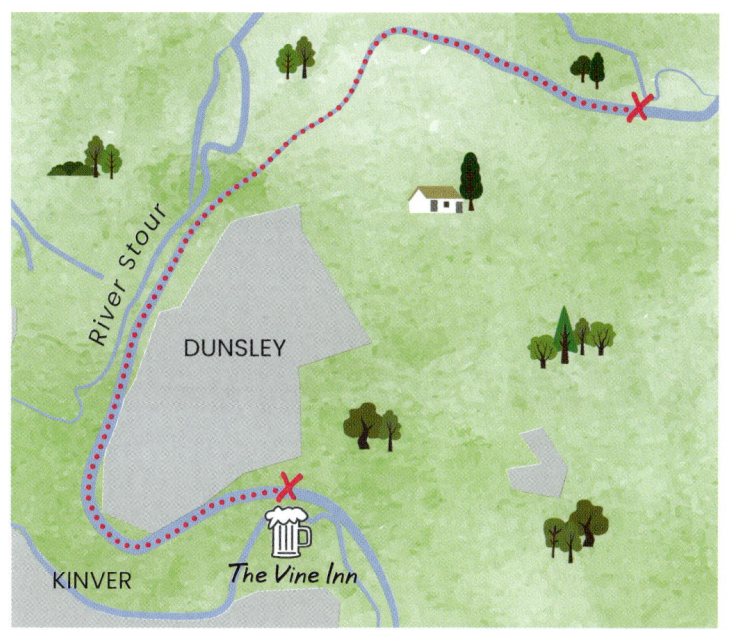

past bright grassy fields, colourful canal boats and tall trees crowning steep banks, returning for a pizza and a pint in the pub.

Independent paddlers can park on the high street.

Do make time for a walk into the landscapes of Kinver Edge, a National Trust site on a sandstone ridge, with an Iron Age hillfort and old cave houses built into the rock with neat green front doors, and chimneys protruding up through the rock.

◗ Details

Hire kayaks at The Vine with River Severn Canoes (*riverseverncanoes.co.uk*). For the pub, see (*thevine-kinver.co.uk*). For info on the village, see (*stourbridge.com/kinver*); for what to see and do on the canals, and their history (*canalrivertrust.org.uk*); more places to paddle and this route (*gopaddling.info/canals/staffordshire-and-worcestershire-canal*).

◗ Make a weekend of it

A 13th-century manor house turned hotel, Dunsley Hall (*dunsleyhallhotel.co.uk*) has gorgeous gardens. The rooms are furnished with flowery curtains, swags and dark pine furniture, but there's a fun smokehouse, Harleys (*harleyssmokehouse.co.uk*), on site, and a conservatory bar.

ABOVE: Weeping willow at the Stourport end of the canal (photo: iStock).

Shropshire/Worcestershire

27 River Severn: Bridgnorth to Arley

- 17km (10.5 miles)
- Fun, countryside, quirky
- Canal
- One way
- Licence needed

This trip is such a lovely concept – it involves paddling one way down the River Severn, then catching a steam train back.

River Severn Canoes has popularised the combo and sells it as a trip, or several trips rather, as you can choose different lengths. Its most popular option is from the Shropshire town of Bridgnorth to Arley, probably because of the length – a 17km (10.5 mile) downriver paddle of about four hours – and the fact that they arrange things so tickets on the Severn Valley Railway (*svr.co.uk*) can be included for your return journey.

As almost always you can do the trip independently too. It's a good one if you have an inflatable or SUP to roll back up and return on the train.

Halfway (about two hours) along this wide green country river,

THE MIDLANDS

there's a pretty place for a picnic on a small beach at the village of Hampton Load, though the **Unicorn Inn** may well tempt you in for a roast. The word 'loade' is an Old English term for ferry and there has been one here – now cable drawn – for four centuries.

Finishing in Upper Arley in Worcestershire, the trip has the possibility of another traditional pub, the 500-year-old **The Harbour**, which sometimes has live music and quizzes. When you are ready, take a train ride back to the start (you leave the hired canoes here).

Bridgnorth is an interesting place, with half of the settlement called 'High Town' up on a sandstone ridge, and the other half called 'Low Town'. Both are linked by a cliff railway. **The Boatyard** is a great summer hang out, with a riverside patio.

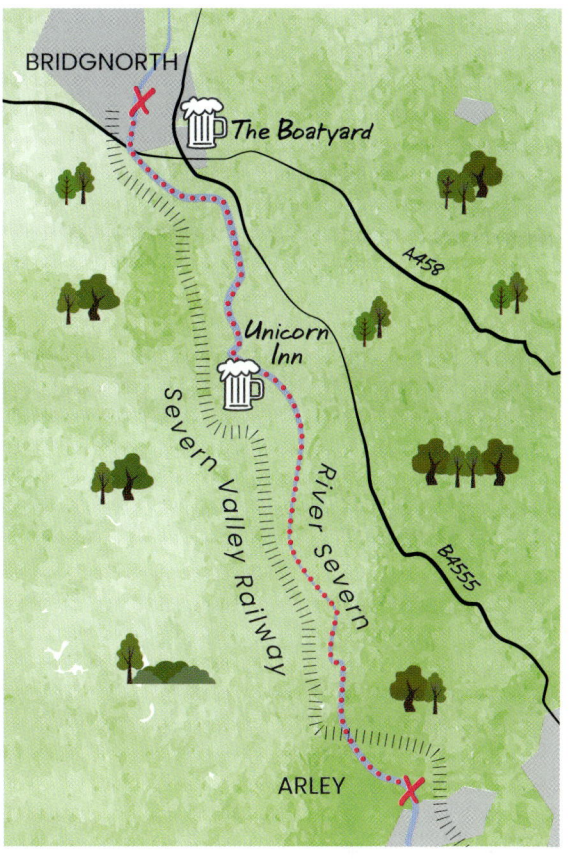

▶ Details

Book this trip with River Severn Canoes (*riverseverncanoes.co.uk*), which also offers a few SUP lessons and trips, and multi-day adventures.

Alternatively, Shropshire Raft Tours (*shropshirerafttours.co.uk*) offers kayak, canoe and SUP hire, and runs trips such as an 11km (7 mile) paddle from Coalport to Bridgnorth, including a shuttle from the latter. The company recommends breakfast at **The Brewery Inn** (*breweryinn.co.uk*) in Coalport beforehand. For info, see the tourist board website (*visitshropshire.co.uk*), and Paddle UK's page (*gopaddling.info/rivers/river-severn*). For the pubs, see (*unicornhamptonloade.co.uk*), (*theharbourarley.co.uk*) and (*facebook.com/boatyard.bridgnorth*).

▶ Alternative route

One of several alternative routes with this company involves carrying on to Bewdley, a total of 22.5km (14 miles) paddling. They

OPPOSITE: Paddle one way along the River Severn, then take the steam train back (photo: iStock).

CLOCKWISE FROM BELOW: Canadian canoes make for a stable, gentle ride; for those looking for a longer paddle, continue this route to Bewdley; the bridge in Bridgnorth (all photos: iStock).

recommend finishing up at **The Mug House** (*mughousebewdley. co.uk*), close to the river and the point where you leave your hired canoes. In the 18th century, when it was built, the term 'Mug House' meant 'ale house' and a characterful wooden-beamed and firelit interior remains. Although the bedrooms and menu are somewhat dated (though fresh fish is delivered daily for fish dishes), the riverfront garden is transporting – Mediterranean in feel with its vines and wisteria.

▶ Make a weekend of it

The Unicorn Inn in Hampton Loade does B&B with nine quite basic rooms, plus two self-catering holiday flats, a caravan and campsite. A bit posher and more unusual is The Hundred House (*hundredhouse.co.uk*) in Norton. It has magical, flower-filled gardens and ten rooms, seven of which have swings hanging from their thick beams. The rooms also include four posters, half testers, chandeliers and florals.

BELOW: Bridgnorth, as viewed across the River Severn (photo: iStock).

Shropshire

28 River Severn: Montford Bridge to Shrewsbury

- 19.3km (12 miles)
- Bucolic, urban, winding
- River
- One way
- Licence needed

Mighty and muddy, the River Severn is, at 354km (220 miles), Great Britain's longest river. One of the country's great arteries, it charges through the Midlands after bubbling up in the Cambrian Mountains in Wales. The cities of Shrewsbury, Worcester, Gloucester and Bristol were established on its banks by the Romans and Saxons who used the river, an important trading route by medieval times. It eventually pours into the Bristol Channel, where it forms an 8km (5 mile) wide estuary. Such scale and power can be an intimidating prospect when it comes to paddling it, and some sections are indeed tricky for the inexperienced. But this attractive 19.3km (12 mile) route through

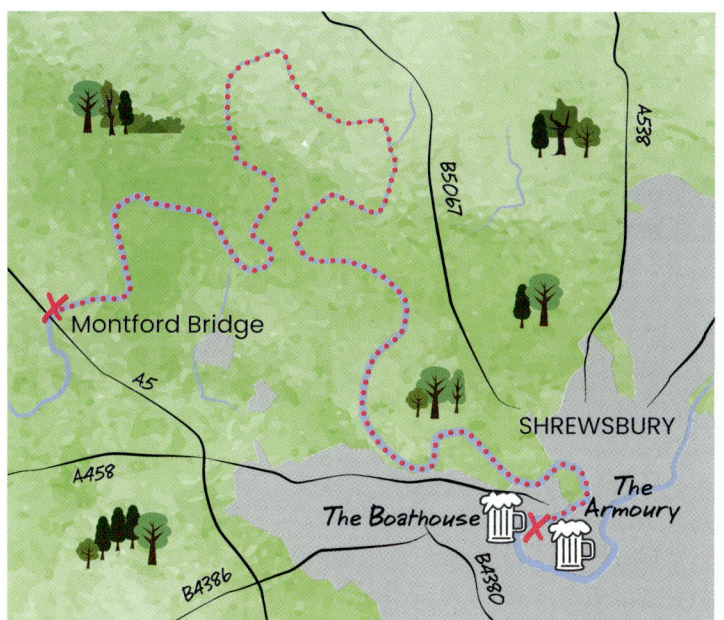

Shrewsbury is straightforward and beginner-friendly, as you go with the flow through a gorgeous green section, ending at a wonderful pub.

Starting north-west of the attractive Shropshire town, you'll enjoy an easy paddle of about 4–5 hours, depending on conditions (and the size of your guns). The river here forms a looping, mad doodle, ribboning back on itself through dramatically tall woodland. Peace among the kingfishers gives way to beery celebration in the lively town centre at the end. Even on a dull drizzly day, I loved it. I went with Hire A Canoe, which describes this route as suitable for beginners, families and dogs. They take paddlers by minibus from Shrewsbury to their base beside the start point, Montford Bridge. This bridge was the first to be designed by the famed civil engineer Thomas Telford, who went on to design some 40 or so more in Shropshire, plus significant other infrastructure projects that transformed the nation. His first attempt, built by convict labour with three elliptical stone arches, is a pretty little charmer. The slipway here isn't public; it's on land owned by the Wingfield Caravan Park, but anyone can launch with their own kit if they pay a fee (currently £1).

Kieran Johnson, Hire A Canoe's founder, provided thorough

OPPOSITE: The English Bridge in Shrewsbury (photo: iStock).

BELOW: The start point at Montford Bridge.

CLOCKWISE FROM TOP LEFT: Arriving at the Boathouse Inn is a thrill; in places the river is wide and green; the Boathouse Inn is always packed on a sunny day (photo: the Boathouse).

guidance and settled me into a nifty touring canoe to paddle the route by myself.

Setting out under the bridge, you're immediately aware of the force of this wide and powerful river, which has the most voluminous flow of all those in England and Wales. It's impressive, but not in a scary way. Kieran told me this section, upriver from the big cities, is surprisingly clean and he often swims the route. Water-crowfoot grows, and sometimes otters appear.

After passing the point where the River Perry joins from the left, there's a shallow section to dodge, and a gravel bank on the right where the water whisks you around a bit. Then the river makes a huge horseshoe loop around the Isle Estate, 8km (5 miles) around, almost circling back on itself. Poachers used to escape being chased by running their coracles across the land at the narrowest point here.

Trees hang over the water from steep cliffs, making the river a deep green gully, where buzzards sometimes soar overhead. The flow is interesting – at times fast and foamy, at times seemingly still as a mirror, but when you look up you realise the landscape is passing at a pace. Weeds snake close to the surface. Geese, herons and unusual brown-headed ducks join the party. At one point, three swans took off from the water, splashing ahead of me then flying over so closely I was buffeted by wing-flapped air. A kingfisher pinballed ahead between the banks for half an hour. Fat raindrops made a scattering of bubbles across the toffee-coloured water. Paddling alone, I felt deliciously lost in nature.

Before Shrewsbury, high on a hillside on the right is a grand red house that was Charles Darwin's birthplace and childhood home (*darwinbirthplacetrust.com*).

The Severn continues to loop and wiggle as you enter the city centre – the whole town is tucked into a big bend. Passing under the cable-stayed Frankwell Footbridge, then Welsh Bridge, you'll paddle alongside the beginnings of Quarry Park, a 29-acre parkland home to the flower-filled sunken garden masterpiece, The Dingle.

Finally, just before the green Port Hill Suspension Bridge, you reach the **Boathouse Inn** with a huge outdoor beer terrace by the water. Pull up at the pontoon, or, if you hired with Hire A Canoe, ditch your steed on the left bank and cross the bridge on foot. On a summer's day it will be rammed, as it may well be inside on colder days, where fires and local guest ales will warm you up. Try regulars from the Salopian brewery, HPA Wye Valley and more, and, if you come in August try to catch the pub's Gin Fest, with a pop-up bar in the garden, or in October, the sausage and cider fest. **The Armoury** is another great waterside boozer in a high-ceilinged red-brick building with good cocktails and cask ales.

▶ Details

Hire A Canoe (*hireacanoe.com*) includes a minibus transfer from Frankwell car park in Shrewsbury to the start point at Montford Bridge. See (*gopaddling.info/rivers/river-severn*). For the pubs, see (*boathouseshrewsbury.co.uk*) and (*brunningandprice.co.uk/armoury*).

▶ Make a weekend of it

Shrewsbury's a great place to spend a little longer. It's an affluent town of pubs, bars and interesting shops (including SUP shop Wake2o), as well as historic landmarks such as the spectacular medieval streets of Grope Lane, Fish Gate and the Traitors Gate. Stay at the chic Lion + Pheasant (*lionandpheasant.co.uk*), a smart contemporary but characterful inn near the river and the Thomas Telford-designed, five arched English Bridge. Light grey wooden-beamed rooms accompany a fantastic fine dining restaurant doing artful plates and good wines. In June the city hosts the Vanlife Festival (*thevanlifefestival.co.uk*) celebrating campervanning, during which many people take to the water. It's also great fun to come for Guy Fawkes night, when paddlers watch the fireworks show from the river.

South of Shrewsbury, Featherdown Farms (*featherdown.co.uk/england/upper-shadymoor-farm-shropshire*) has a waterside option at Shadymoor Farm, with kayaks and paddleboards on site.

▶ Alternative routes

Paddle another section further upriver from Montford Bridge, where the village of Edgerley near Oswestry is home to the Royal Hill Inn (*royalhill.co.uk*), just over the road from the river, with settees and big fireplaces.

OPPOSITE: This route on the River Severn is a gorgeous adventure through green, high-sided banks.

BELOW: The Armoury is another appealing waterside drinking spot.

Cheshire

29 Chester and the River Dee

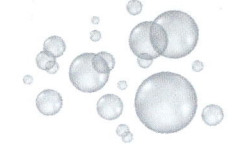

- 3.2km (2 miles)
- City, historic, architecture
- River
- Out and back
- Licence needed

Why Chester hasn't really made it big in mini-break territory yet is a head scratcher – the cathedral city has a Roman amphitheatre and Roman walls, Tudor timber-framed buildings, and even its own unique two-tier, timbered shopping arcades, The Rows, the originals of which date back to the 13th century (though most are Victorian copies). It's on a par with York or Bath.

Like those cities, Chester is defined by its river, the Dee, a mighty vein that flows in and out of Wales and Cheshire, rising in Snowdonia, passing through Lake Bala and out to the Irish Sea. The river is increasingly appreciated by paddlers, perambulators and pub goers too.

Dee River Kayaking runs river trips paddling from its base in Sandy Lane Park. The route runs downstream past Chester Meadows, the university, Chester Castle, Chester's racecourse (the

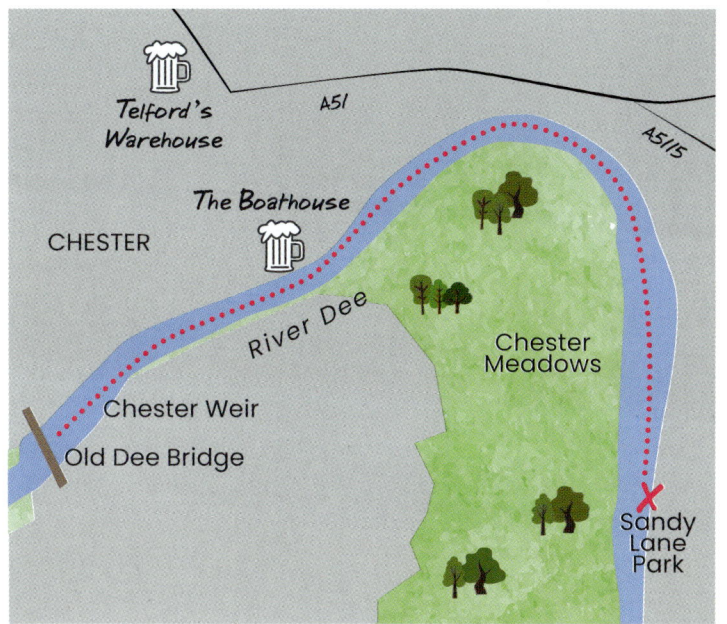

country's oldest) and under Old Dee Bridge up to the weir, where most people will end their trip and turn back. Those who book a whitewater session can learn to play there.

Independent paddlers can park at Sandy Lane Park (free for four hours at time of publication), which has ramps to access the water. It's about 30–45 minutes downriver from here to the weir, which shouldn't be tackled without expertise because it features a 3m (10ft) drop and strong currents that can be very dangerous. Just before the weir you'll pass under a suspension bridge and see several yellow buoys which indicate it's time to turn around. The best riverside spot for a pint afterwards is **The Boathouse**, with a floating restaurant terrace by the water just on the east side of the city centre, serving cask ales.

OPPOSITE: The River Dee running through Chester (photo: iStock).

▶ Details

Book tours and hire with Dee River Kayaking (*deeriverkayaking.com*), which also provides information for independent paddlers on its website, and has a dedicated page about the weir (*deeriverkayaking.com/paddleguides-chesterweir*). Direct Kayaks (*wrexhamkayakhire.co.uk*) also offers rental at Sandy Lane and other bases on the river, such as Ecclestone. See Paddle UK's website (*gopaddling.info/rivers/river-dee*).

ABOVE: Chester's riverside is lined with interesting old buildings (photo: iStock).

▶ Make a weekend of it

For a luxurious boutique Chester stay, try Wildes Hotel (*wildeschester.com*) for creative dining and a spa or Oddfellows (*oddfellowschester.com*), which has some quirky loft rooms. The Boathouse (*theboathousechester.co.uk*) also has bedrooms if you want to be right by the water. Chester usually hosts a paddleboard festival in June (*chesterpaddleboardfestival.uk*).

▶ Alternative route

Another paddle to the pub trip takes place on the canal, a 90-minute paddle west to **Telford's Warehouse** (*telfordswarehousechester.com*) a bar and restaurant in a Georgian brick industrial building designed by Thomas Telford. Built over the water so canal boat cargo could be unloaded into it, the solid building stays true to its industrial past with clunky artefacts displayed on the walls and a glass front overlooking the water. It was only converted into a pub in 1980 and has run in its current incarnation since 1993, offering CAMRA-approved cask ales, roasts, burgers, pizzas and rock and roll. It often hosts gigs, with Coldplay, Courtney Pine and Nitin Sawney among those who have played there.

More great paddles in the Midlands

BIRMINGHAM

It's long been dubbed the 'Venice of the Midlands', which never fails to make me smile. While Birmingham's canals might not have the romance and beauty of La Serenissima, you can't argue they're not a fun and interesting place to paddle. An hour-long easy guided kayak trip, called Paddle, Pizza and Pint (*roundhousebirmingham.org.uk/product/paddle-pizza-and-a-pint*), takes a loop north of Ladywood. It's run by the Roundhouse, a Grade II listed venue and charity, which also offers themed historic walking tours. The trip includes pizza and a drink at **The Distillery** (*thedistillerybirmingham.co.uk*), a red-brick converted warehouse by the canal that sells the Roundhouse's own gin.

LOUGHBOROUGH TO LEICESTER ON THE RIVER SOAR

Linking these two major cities, the Soar also connects several decent pubs for a day out. In Barrow Upon Soar, **The Moorings** (*themoorings.pub*), which started as a coal store but turned boozer in 1980, has a large riverside beer garden. Going south, next comes the **Navigation Inn** (*facebook.com/thenavigationbarrow*), with good bitters and ales on tap. Next door

BELOW: Birmingham's canal system has seen it likened to Venice (photo: iStock).

ABOVE: Boating on the Trent and Mersey canal (photo: iStock).

is **Barrow Boating** (*barrowboating.co.uk*), which hires out kayaks, SUPs, boats and pedalos in every shape from flamingo to VW Beetle. Also try **The Waterside Inn** (*watersidemountsorrel.co.uk*), built in 1795 by a lock between the river and the Union Canal Mountsorrel, for local Leicestershire cask ales. Let's Get Lost (*letsgetlost.uk/pub-trips*) runs dedicated pub paddle trips on this route, starting from Proctors Park in Barrow Upon Soar and lasting four hours. Paddle UK (*gopaddling.info/rivers/river-soar*) has more route info for independent paddlers.

WILLINGTON, DERBYSHIRE

With a great beer garden backing onto the Trent and Mersey canal, the 150-year old **Dragon** pub (*thedragonatwillington.co.uk*) in Willington is a favourite of boaters, hikers and paddlers, who come to try a pint of Boot Beer, or even one of their famous Champagne breakfasts. Two igloos, heaped with sheepskins, provide covered garden seating, and there's a snug for muddy-booted boozers, as well as a conservatory and dining room. Stay over in the pub's rooms or holiday cottage. Willington in south Derbyshire is home to the county's largest marina, Mercia Marina (*merciamarina.co.uk*), with shops and cafes. A fun option is to paddle from one to the other, between the pub and marina.

The Northeast

Yorkshire

30 River Ouse: Bishopthorpe to Acaster Malbis

- 6.4km (4 miles)
- Historic, bucolic, relaxing
- River
- Out and back
- Licence needed

South of the magnificent Viking city of York, 5km (3 miles) down the River Ouse, lies the aspirational and villagey suburb of Bishopthorpe. It was so named in 1226 when Archbishop of York, Walter de Grey, bought a manor house here, which transmogrified into the palace that stands today. It's from this chichi enclave of posh cafes and shops that you'll set out on this invigorating paddle, downriver to **The Ship Inn** in the leafy village of Acaster Malbis.

In Bishopthorpe, the place to launch from is **The Boatyard**, a mixed-purpose private marina with canoe and kayak hire, berths for boats, accommodation, a beer garden and a slipway. There's also quite a snazzy place to eat and drink, Bosun's Restaurant, in a modern octagonal building on stilts, with glitzy interiors hung with green foliage, and glass all the way around to make the most of the river views. Blackened salt-baked celeriac, and sticky

aromatic pork belly with a black pudding crumb are the sorts of things you'll find on the menu.

You could just call this your pub, paddle for ten minutes here then return to the beer garden – if the sun's out and the cocktails are flowing, who would blame you? But there's more to see, so don't be tempted to be lazy.

Setting out downriver, you have at your back the grandeur of the Archbishop of York's waterside palace and, 5km (3 miles) upstream, the spires and red-brick buildings of York. You might want to paddle 200m (660ft) upriver first for a closer look at the archbishop's digs. Very occasionally it is opened for public tours, but these get booked up years in advance – none are currently available for at least two years – so enjoy getting to survey the Gothic

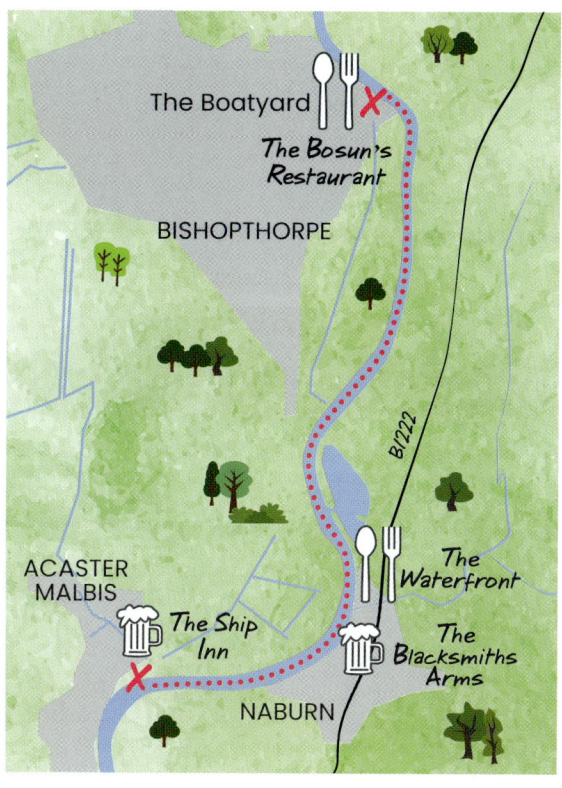

red-brick exterior from the water. It's more than most people will see.

Setting out at 9am (a bargain £15 for two hours' kayak hire from the Boatsheds) I almost immediately saw a kingfisher and, as the rural landscapes unfolded, I was glad to wipe the cobwebs away with a paddle.

Continuing on your course downstream, you'll pass some unusual house boats moored to the grassy banks, some messy and ramshackle, some super slick black timber numbers hung with house plants, then pass under an old railway swing bridge.

Continue through a green section lined with weeping willows, which bring some froth to the banks. Then comes the village of Naburn on the east side, home to York Marina, which has a coffee shop and bar, **The Waterfront**, serving beer, wine, cocktails and coffee in a smart conservatory. Naburn's pub, the **Blacksmith's Arms**, is an easy stop too, as there's a slipway just in front of it.

Onwards then to the Ship. It took me about 30 minutes to get there altogether in fairly fast flowing water without stopping. The

OPPOSITE: The calm River Ouse heading south from Bishopsthorpe.

CLOCKWISE FROM BELOW: The Ship Inn in Acaster Malbis; hopefully that includes paddlers; the pub's beer garden.

pub has landing jetties, but I found these a little high above the water on my trip so prepare to stretch or find an alternative further up the banks. This wide and powerful river can be prone to bursting its banks in heavy rain. Indeed, our target pub was closed for nine months in 2008/9 due to flood damage.

The Ship is a fine, wood-beamed beauty of a pub, dating to the 17th century, with a neat grassy low-walled garden with beer tables by the water and a traditional interior. No flashy flounces, no naffness, it's just a good honest pub. Several ghostly encounters have been reported here, so watch out for a mysterious grey figure, and the fire that has been known to light itself. Warm up with a hot drink and maybe a game of darts or pool, then all you have to do is paddle back.

▶ Details

For information see the Paddle UK site (*gopaddling.info/rivers/river-ouse-in-yorkshire*). Hire kayaks and canoes at The Boatyard (*the-boatyard.co.uk*). Stop for an easy drink at the Blacksmith's Arms (*facebook.com/naburnvillage*). Get a closer look at Bishopthorpe Palace from the water (*archbishopofyork.org/archbishop-york/about-bishopthorpe-palace*).

▶ Make a weekend of it

The Ship Inn (*shipinn-acastermalbis.com*) has B&B rooms. The Boatyard has quite basic cabins and houseboats to stay in, plus a drinks and snacks hut, Wild Goat Coffee, doing great greasy breakfast baps, lunchtime pizzas and – oh lordy yes – cheesy chips. York Marina (*yorkmarina.co.uk*) offers smarter 'floating cabin' accommodation, while Poplar Farm (*poplarfarm-caravans.co.uk*) has camping and a cottage. Or stay to the south-east of the city at Pool Bridge Farm (*poolbridge.co.uk*) which offers wild swimming, outdoor barrel sauna sessions, and glamping. Don't miss going into the centre of York to the famous Jorvik Viking Centre and to ramble the higgledy-piggledy streets, such as the Shambles, with its overhanging timber-framed upper floors, and any number of Harry Potter-inspired stores. Walking the city walls is another favourite for visitors, along with ghost tours and river cruises. Great city centre hotels include Number 1 By GuestHouse (*guesthousehotels.co.uk*) or the grand, wood-panelled Grays Court Hotel (*grayscourtyork.com*) near York Minster.

BELOW: The river closer in to the city of York.

North Yorkshire

31 Staithes Harbour and the Cod and Lobster

- 1.6km (1 mile)
- Coastal, historic, charming
- Sea
- Out and back
- No licence needed

One of the loveliest fishing villages in the entire country, higgledy-piggledy, uppy-downy Staithes on the North Yorkshire coast is where several proud worlds collide. A small fleet of cobbles (fishing boats) still bob and bustle in the harbour. The village wears its heritage as a badge, yet an arty crowd thrives here too. Tiny galleries and shops are dotted through its colourful, steep and narrow streets and alleyways – one of these, Dog Loup, is claimed to be Britain's narrowest at just 39cm (15.4in) wide.

A paddle out from the harbour here is a delight. A wide pond-like section protected by the harbour wall is good for a beginners' splash about. You might then head a little way around to the just-deep-enough and picturesque Staithes Beck on the north side of town, or paddle out along the coastline.

If conditions allow and you have the skills and experience, the sea is your oyster, but as always, be extremely mindful of winds and tides. Avoid going out if there is any offshore wind and take all the safety precautions outlined at the beginning of the book.

BELOW: Cottages and cliffs above Staithes Beck.

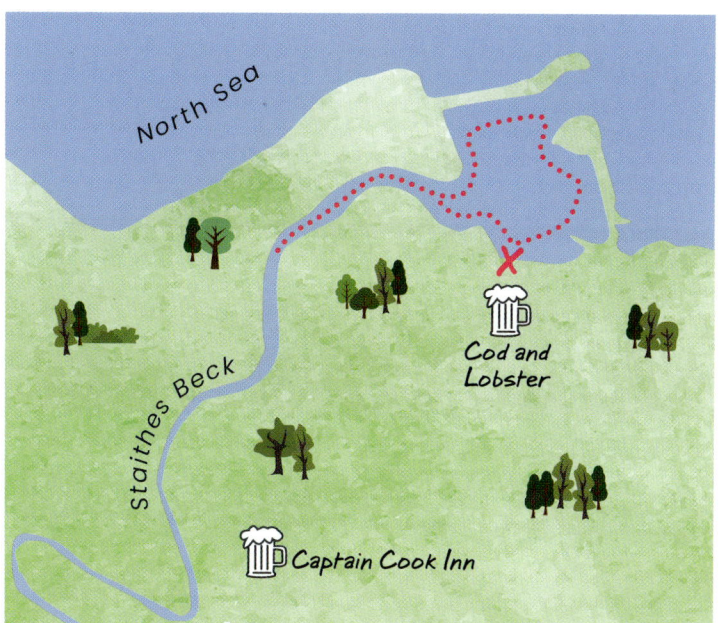

Paddle to your heart's content then return to the town's fantastic seaside pub, the **Cod and Lobster**. Locals and tourists, drinkers and gourmands, jostle at tables packed into the small indoor spaces whose walls are hung with old photos. If the sun's out, grab a seat on the terrace between the street and the sea for some people- and paddler-watching.

No prizes for guessing the signature dish: cod (oven baked with potato rosti and samphire) with lobster, a grilled half, accompanied by a bisque. No one's going to punch you for ordering the lasagne but the delicious fish and seafood dishes are highly recommended.

Wild stormy seas have caused damage in the past – the pub is the last line of defence against the North Sea, they say, and in 1953 the front was torn off and washed away. The sign that reads 'in rough weather use other door' means it, or you may get sloshed by seawater on your way out. On those days, a fire roars inside, and equally warming is the gin list, which is insanely long. So too is the whisky list, come to mention it. And the rum. Maybe some of the swashbuckling, grog-guzzling, smuggling spirit remains among those living about this area. The most famous local around these parts was Captain James Cook, who was apprenticed to a grocer here as a teenager in 1745, and where the

BELOW: Rocks around Staithes.

CLOCKWISE FROM TOP RIGHT: Lobster pots piled at the harbour; the steep and charming streets of Staithes; outside the Cod and Lobster.

sight of the sea inspired his pelagic life. Related information and memorabilia, plus photographs and documents concerning the area's fishing and ironstone industries, can be seen in The Staithes Museum (*staithes-museum.org.uk*). At the top of the village, The **Captain Cook Inn**, the Cod and Lobster's sister pub, pumps its own real ale, Northern Navigator, made by the North Yorkshire Brewery, and has bedrooms.

▶ Details

Park at Bank Top Car Park and carry your kit down to the water. The uphill return is harder so alternatively, drop your stuff and drive back up the hill to park. For a little more information, see (*paddling.com/paddle/locations/staithes*). At the time of writing there were no local hire places here. For the pubs, see (*captaincookinn.co.uk*) and (*codandlobster.co.uk*).

▶ Make a weekend of it

The Captain Cook Inn has simple seaview rooms, or there are four super stylish ones at The Endeavour B&B (*endeavour-staithes.co.uk*), which does a mean breakfast. The owners' names couldn't be more fitting: Caroline and Cameron Paddle.

BELOW: The Cod and Lobster's terrace overlooking Staithes harbour.

More great paddles in North Yorkshire

SALTBURN-BY-THE-SEA

The seaside resort of Saltburn is a jolly spot with colourful beach huts, a beginner-friendly surf school, and old-fashioned attractions from a pier to a vintage cliff tramway taking people up and down between the beach and town. Bring your own kit and stay close to the shore, paddling alongside the beach, unless you're a confident sea-paddler. At the eastern end, below Old Saltburn, **The Ship** (*greeneking.co.uk/pubs/north-yorkshire/ship-inn*) is a history-enshrined pub with an outdoor bar and seating in an open-sided cabin overlooking the waves. There's bar food and takeaway fish and chips. The interiors, jazzed up in 2023, feature terracotta floor tiles, marine blue panelling, floral chairs and bold patterned wallpapers – a far cry from its 18th century origins. It's the oldest pub in what was once a fishing village, whose former landlord was known as 'King of the Smugglers'. Until 1881 the pub also doubled as the village mortuary.

RUNSWICK BAY

The long sandy beach at Runswick is amazing enough to have been voted Britain's Best in 2020 by the *Sunday Times*, chosen by

BELOW: Saltburn-by-the-Sea's beach and pier.

the travel writer Chris Haslam, who tours the country's beaches each year on his quest. He described it as 'a beach close to perfection'. Alas Barefoot Kayaking, which had a base here offering hire and trips, wasn't operating at the time of writing, but it's a lovely, relatively sheltered spot for those with their own gear. You still need to be very careful of offshore winds and follow safety protocols.

On the front, the **Royal Hotel** (runswickbay.com/the-royal) pub has a beer garden, an open fire and changing local ales, or at the top of the village, up the incredibly steep road that leads down to the sea (don't drive it, there's nowhere to park), the simple but stylish **Runswick Bay Hotel** (therunswickbay.com) has a menu of fishy bites, burgers and pizza, and six chic grey bedrooms upstairs. The Cleveland Way runs through the car park. Very competent sea kayakers could paddle from Runswick to Staithes, about 5 or 6km (3 or 4 miles) one way.

WHITBY

Leave the Dracula-related gift shops and mazey streets full of pubs and fish and chip shops behind and paddle away from Whitby Harbour inland up the River Esk to the village of Ruswarp. Whitby Surf (whitbysurf.co.uk) hires out SUPs and kayaks. Go from Whitby an hour before high tide, have a drink at traditional **The Bridge Inn** (thebridgeinnruswarp.co.uk), then head back down with the changed tide. Or do it the other way round, and hire a kayak from Ruswarp Pleasure Boats (ruswarppleasureboats.co.uk) to visit Whitby with its many waterside pubs. These include The Golden Lion, The Endeavour, The Pier Inn, The Ship Inn, The Fleece... the list goes on.

ABOVE: Colourful beach huts at Saltburn-by-the-Sea.

BELOW: The Runswick Bay Hotel has chic bedrooms and access to the Cleveland Way.

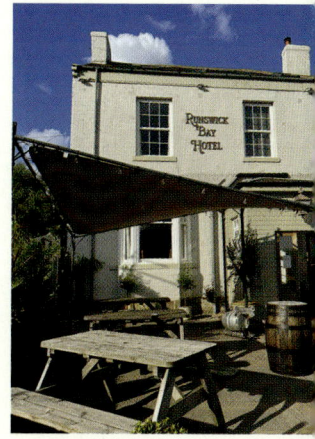

MORE GREAT PADDLES IN NORTH YORKSHIRE

County Durham/North Yorkshire

32 River Tees: Stockton to Yarm

- 12km (7.5 miles)
- Rural, farmland, challenge
- River
- Out and back
- Licence needed

Darkly brown as gravy and velvety as Guinness, the peaty River Tees flows through an alluring part of the northeast countryside, rising in the North Pennines at North Fell and winding east, until a final churn through the once thriving industrial area of Teesside, east of Middlesbrough, and into the North Sea.

In the west, rapids and sections of whitewater thrill paddlers with the skills to enjoy them, while the middle sections, almost down to the Tees Barrage at built-up Middlesbrough, are wide idyllic bends through glorious countryside and characterful towns. The last of these is Yarm, your objective on this lengthy paddle upstream and back.

I have a personal connection to the under-rated Tees, as my grandparents lived close to it: my maternal Granny and Grampy, in the sweet village of Gainsford, where I spent happy childhood days paddling (of the little-feet-in-the-water variety) and fishing for minnows from a beach of smooth round stones. My dad's side hailed from Hartlepool, raising him in Billingham, an unattractive industrial town adjoining Middlesbrough – two very different places showcasing very different aspects of one river. I returned for the first time in years for this paddle, which several local paddle groups and guides recommended to me.

The place to park, with easy public access to the river, is Preston Park Museum and Grounds (*prestonparkmuseum.co.uk*) in Stockton. The site features a recreation Victorian street, playground, cafe and walled garden, if you have time to visit. Park at the closest end to the river and carry your kit over the sloping grass down to the water's edge, where there's a jetty to launch from.

I paddleboarded this route alone in summer and found it fairly easy-going heading upriver against the tide, but check conditions. David Hopkins of Tees Outdoors, who runs trips there, warned me that it can 'flow at speed if the river is up'.

Heading south, you'll pass covetable large houses on the banks, shaded by towering trees, then you'll come out into open, sheep-dotted farmland.

After some glorious stretches where the banks are thick with tall trees, you'll come into Yarm, crossed by a viaduct with 43 arches. It's just before this, on the right-hand, eastern bank that you need to be for the pub. There are jetties slightly hidden in the undergrowth, or you can get out on the left bank and carry your board across the road. To be honest, it's not that easy and I ended up scrambling out through mud.

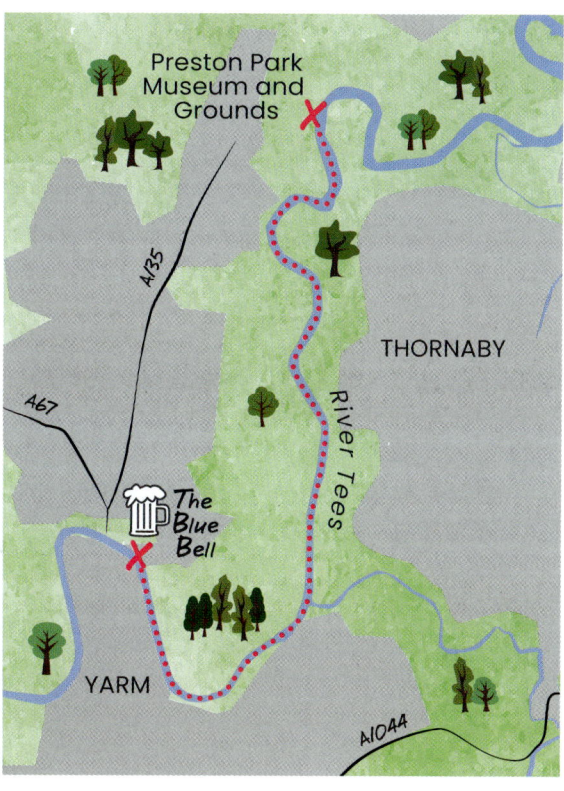

OPPOSITE: The wide and graceful River Tees.

32 RIVER TEES

TOP TO BOTTOM: The bridge at Yarm; The Blue Bell pub; heading downriver from Yarm.

The Blue Bell has stood here since the 1700s when it was a coaching inn. It remains a friendly and down-to-earth pub: a big white building with benches in the riverside garden (a little overgrown), an outdoor terraces (a little scruffy) and lovely staff. On the menu are a wide range of variations on the area's famous 'Teesside parmesans' or 'parmos' – a filthily indulgent dish of breaded chicken topped with bechamel sauce and cheese that seems to have gained global fame. Scoff one of those and you'll be glad you've got the whole return paddle still to do, though it's a lot faster and easier as it's downstream.

▶ Details

Tees Outdoors (*teesoutdoors.co.uk/activities*) tailor-makes paddle adventures, and can throw in other activities from campcraft and gorge scrambles to multi-day trips with camping, bivouacking and wild camping. Canal River Trust has details and a map of the Tees Barrage to Yarm canoe trail, and there's car parking and water access at the barrage (*canalrivertrust.org.uk*). For more info, see Paddle UK's website (*gopaddling.info/rivers/river-tees*). For the pub, see (*facebook.com/TheBlueBellatYarm*).

▶ Make a weekend of it

Near Croft, upriver, the five star country hotel Rockcliffe Hall (*rockliffehall.com*) is pretty posh, with a golf course and a huge spa that has an outdoor hot tub and pool.

▶ Alternative routes

A popular 8.9km (5.5 mile) paddle runs from Croft downriver to Neasham, for the Fox and Hounds pub (*foxandhoundsneashampub.co.uk*). There are numerous other places to get in (*gopaddling.info/rivers/river-tees*), plus lively water and rapids around Barnard Castle and Cotherstone. 'Barney', as it's known locally, is worth a mooch for its ruined castle overlooking the Tees Gorge, operated by English Heritage, and its antiques shops. Experienced whitewater paddlers can try the course at the Tees Barrage International White Water Centre (*tbiwwc.com/activities/paddlesports*), which also offers beginners' lessons in SUP and kayaking.

Northumberland

33 River Coquet: Amble to Warkworth

—	6.4km (4 miles)
●	Rural, town, coastal
～	Tidal river
=	One way
▪	No licence needed

This one is a paddle of two halves, combining a coastal fishing village and a charming inland medieval town, linked by the tidal tail end of the River Coquet.

These two Northumbrian towns are both very charming yet very different, each of them worthy places to visit in their own right, and with good options for a tipple. Which way around you do this route is up to you, but it helps to go with the tide. There are more pubs in Warkworth, but better food options in Amble-on-Sea.

The latter is a colourful coastal village that has the look and feel of a Scandinavian or Icelandic fishing harbour, with corrugated metal buildings in muted colours, a fishmarket with

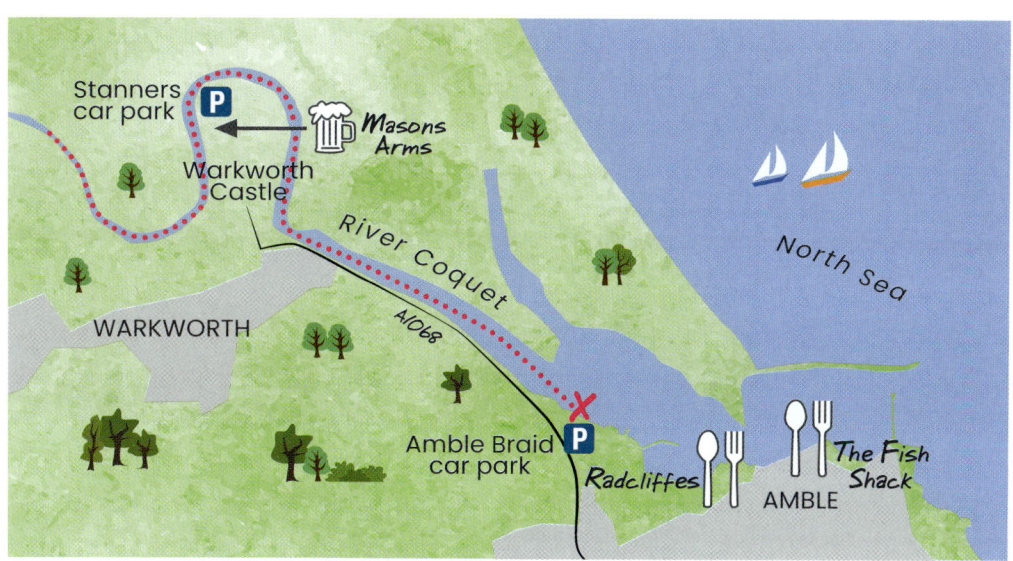

tanks full of lobsters, and a breezy redeveloped area on the waterfront to potter around, with wooden stalls selling sweets and gifts. At the end of the line of vendors, **The Fish Shack** is a slick and glossy spot for excellent fresh fish dishes, platters of Lindisfarne oysters, lobster and North Shields dressed crab, and a bar serving drinks until 9pm. Interesting too is **Radcliffes**, a hip looking space serving great breakfasts of avo smash and veggie haggis rolls, German sausage and loaded fries, plus a fantastic variety of beers, for after your paddle. So depending on tide times you might have breakfast or lunch before departing upriver from Amble, or feast on your return.

Best for river access is Amble Braid Car Park, near Amble Marina and the Coquet Yacht Club. Put in here and head upriver towards Warkworth, whose imposing medieval castle, once home to the Dukes of Northumberland, is visible standing guard on an outcrop above the town.

Beware that halfway between the two towns is a substantial weir, so it's best to set out 90 minutes or less before high tide to get over it, or you'll need to portage around.

Once in Warkworth, follow the river east as it loops in a horseshoe around the tangle of appealing streets, passing under a road bridge and a medieval stone bridge. It can be quite shallow here so take your time to find the deepest channel through.

If you decide to go the other way, or just want a short paddle

OPPOSITE: Warkworth with its castle and the River Coquet looping through.

BELOW: The Harbour Inn in Amble.

33 RIVER COQUET

CLOCKWISE FROM TOP LEFT: Interesting beers on tap in Radcliffes; The Fish Shack overlooks the sea in Amble; the beer garden of The Masons Arms; a green stretch of the River Coquet upriver from Warkworth.

from Warkworth, Stanners car park is the place to park. There are spaces next to grass where you can pump, a few steps from easy river access from a pebble beach. It's just behind this car park too that you can head up Brewery Lane, straight into the little sheltered beer garden (a tiny yard, really) of the **Masons Arms**. Lovely inside, this cosy charmer has low-ceilings and panelled walls, a fire and built-in seating nooks.

A couple of other pubs lie on the main drag, and if you want a longer paddling route, keep heading upriver out of town, into rural surroundings.

❱ Details

Northside Surf School (*northside-surf-school.co.uk/stand-up-paddle-boarding*) has paddleboard hire; Coquet Shore Base (*coquetshorebase.org.uk*) runs summer kayak trips on the Coquet Estuary. For venues, see (*boathousefoodgroup.co.uk/fish-shack*), (*radcafeamble.com*) and (*themasonsarmswarkworth.co.uk*).

❱ Make a weekend of it

Up near the castle in Warkworth, The Sun Hotel (*thesunhotelwarkworth.co.uk*) is an elegant bolthole, all chandeliers and suits of armour, with a traditional pub attached, the **Castle Brew House**. Crabtree and Crabtree (*crabtreeandcrabtree.com*) has wonderful cottages in the area and across Northumberland.

BELOW: Kayakers head upriver from Amble to Warkworth.

Northumberland

34 Beadnell Bay to Low Newton

- 0.8km (0.5 miles)
- Coastal, invigorating, beautiful
- Sea
- Out and back
- No licence needed

Fringed with gorgeous demerara sands that form a huge wide sheltered sweep, Beadnell Bay is a glorious place to practise your sea-paddling.

Thanks to its perfect halfmoon form, it feels protected even on a windy day. You do still need to be careful and very aware of conditions, not going out in strong offshore winds.

Among Northumberland's many beautiful beaches, Beadnell stands out as a centre for watersports and family fun, with kiteboarding, windsurfing, wakeboarding and paddle sports popular in the waves, and beach games played on the sand. It's a good starting point too for lovely walks in the dunes. This is such a friendly place to paddle: fellow SUPers chatted to me in the car

park, one raving about how he'd only just started paddleboarding but had already experienced cormorants diving under his board as he set out with his young son – the sort of magical moment that keeps us all hooked.

Just 100m (330ft) back from the beach and its large public car park is **The Landing**, a fun surfy café and bar with an Ibiza/Mexican/Pacific coast hippy vibe, with rough plaster walls, oversized raffia lampshades, succulents and dangling foliage. There's live music in the tipi on Sundays.

In front of it, adjacent to the public car park, is the base of KA Adventures (*kaadventuresports.co.uk*) an excellent outfit offering watersports including kitesurfing and SUP rental. It also runs brilliant waterborne tours from here for competent paddleboarders – out to the Farne Islands to snorkel with seals, and down along the coast, with a support rescue RIB and jetski accompanying for safety.

Those with the experience and knowledge to paddle a distance in the sea could do this paddle alone but as with all sea paddles, you need to know what you're doing. Get local advice and be certain the conditions are favourable.

The trip to plump for is to Low Newton. Reach the tiny hamlet by paddling around the curve of the bay to the south, then around the next headland and into the neighbouring bay. The beachside village green is backed by **The Ship**, where paddlers stop for a slap-up lunch. The pub, in a pretty white-washed cottage, has its own micro-brewery by the sea, with phenomenal beers. Try the golden Sandcastles At Dawn or a Sea Dog Stout. The setting is truly special, overlooking a tufty beach of perfect light sand, the coast stretching far into the distance, capped by the dramatic Dunstanburgh castle looming to the south on the other side of Embleton Bay.

OPPOSITE: The Landing at Beadnell Bay.

ABOVE: The Ship at Low Newton.

▶ Details

KA Adventures (*kaadventuresports.co.uk*) offers watersports, SUP hire and lessons on the beach, plus tours including this one. See (*northumberlandcoast-nl.org.uk/kayaking*) for information, and for the venues, see (*northcoastcollective.co.uk/the-landing*) and (*shipinnnewton.co.uk*).

▶ Make a weekend of it

Crabtree and Crabtree (*crabtreeandcrabtree.com*) has gorgeous cottages in the area, or book one of the apartments within the striking Bamburgh Castle (*bamburghcastle.com/accommodation*), or at least go for a visit.

Above Low Newton, a former lookout has been transformed into a four-person holiday home by the National Trust (*nationaltrust.org.uk/holidays/northumberland-north-east/lookout-cottage*).

More fishing villages on the Northumberland coast

CRASTER AND THE JOLLYFISHERMAN

Smoked kippers are what Craster is best known for – the L Robson & Sons smokehouse has been turning the little blighters into soft deliciousness for 130 years.

The fishing village is also the home of the **Jolly Fisherman** (*thejollyfishermancraster.co.uk*), a dark, stylish pub that makes good use of nature's bounty beyond its inky walls and seaview terrace. Overlooking the harbour and with a very well-regarded kitchen, it turns out famously good crab soup, Shetland mussels and Lindisfarne oysters, fish boards, fish pie and – if you must – non-fishy alternatives from chips with beef dripping to bean chilli.

ABOVE: The fishing village of Craster, famed for its smoked kippers (photo: iStock).

Turn up on a summer evening and you're unlikely to get a table so call ahead, or get there early to get in line for the posh fish and chips van outside.

Hire kayaks and SUPs from Adventure Northumberland (*adventurenorthumberland.co.uk*) to explore up and down the coastline a little, nosing into the harbour area but keeping out of the fishermens' way, or book its kayak and coasteering trip and make stops to leap from rocks into gullies.

SEAHOUSES

Bright, colourful, slightly naff and tacky in parts, with a big adventure golf opposite the car park and giant giftshops selling tat, Seahouses is nevertheless well worth your time on account of its incredibly characterful pub.

On Main Street, leading to the harbour, two pubs sit opposite each other like two opposing armies. One, the **Bamburgh Castle Inn** (inncollectiongroup.com/bamburgh-castle-inn) has been smartly done up and is owned by the Inn Collection group, which has several in the northeast and Lake District.

But if it's soul, history and individuality you're after then cross over the road, my friend, for **Ye Olde Ship Inn** (theoldeship.co.uk) a singular old fishermen's pub, which has character in buckets and spades. The decor looks as if a pirate's treasure chest exploded inside. It's the pub of dreams for those whose hearts ache for the days of smugglers and a life at sea. Marine paraphernalia hangs from every inch: lanterns, wheels, framed knots, ship paintings, boards listing the names of the boats that went out. Even the floor is made from pine ship decking. An outdoor terrace overlooks the sea, and there are surprisingly smart and simple bedrooms too. Launch at the harbour, fees apply, and steer clear of tourist boats, paddling out a little way and up or down the coast to see this bustling old harbour town from the water. See (northumberlandcoast-nl.org.uk/kayaking).

BELOW: Craster's The Jolly Fisherman pub has excellent food (photo: iStock).

The Northwest

Cumbria

35 Lake District: Crummock Water and the Kirkstile Inn

- 3 to 6.5 km (2 to 4 miles) flexible
- Mountains, dramatic, peaceful
- Lake
- Out and back
- Licence needed

A short, 3km (2 mile) drive north of Buttermere is beautiful Crummock Water. At one point, prior to the last ice age, the two were conjoined, but rockfalls separated them. Now Crummock runs for 4km (2.5 miles), with Grassmore rising on the west and Mellbreak to the east. It feels at once both starkly isolated, with no buildings in sight, and cosily protected, with tree-shadowed beaches tucked beneath sheep-nibbled grassy verges. The B5289 road runs all along the eastern edge, making it easy to pull in to park in one of the grassy laybys (mind the sheep).

Long hours of slack-jawed gazing await. It's a fabulously scenic place to paddle – untouristy, with little islands and rugged, lumpen hills all around, making it my favourite lake after 40 years

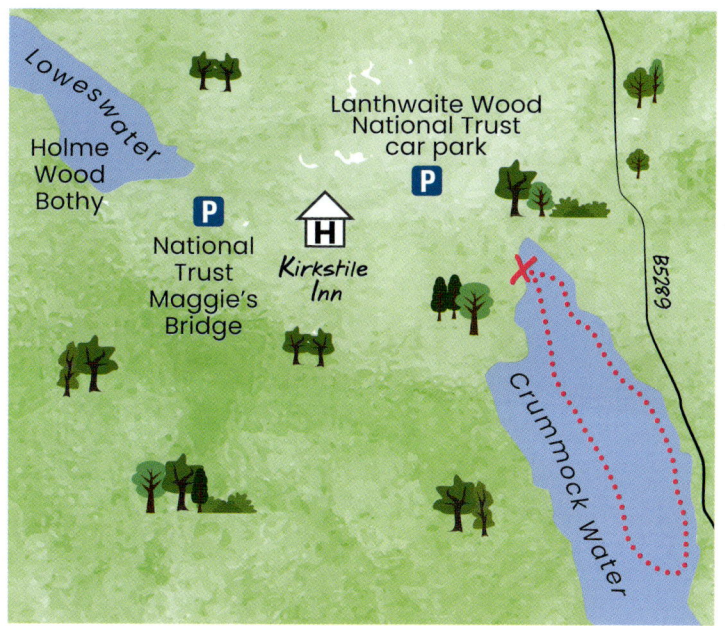

of visiting. It has a special place in my heart as somewhere I played as a child, somewhere my toddler daughter swam across to a little islet, and as the last place I holidayed with my dad before he died. On my most recent visit, my daughter and I ventured out for a magical evening paddle (though strictly it was really bedtime) after a family dinner at the nearby **Kirkstile Inn**. As the sun dipped behind the darkening peaks, we drifted out onto silvery water on our shared paddleboard, bats darting around us, with not a single other soul on the lake. This was in August, and just shows that you can always find peace in the Lakes, whatever the season.

That pub too is, I believe, the national park's finest: fantastic food, staff who really put in the effort to be kind and fun (the barman taught my kids a new game), and its own, unbeatable Loweswater Gold on tap. Firelit snugs will welcome you in from wild weather, and on sunny days you can bed in to the levelled beer garden among the hikers who flock here after conquering the dramatic fells.

Though it's not strictly a waterside pub – there's just over 1.5km (1 mile) to walk between the two – this is a winning combo: the Lake District's best pub and loveliest lake in one excursion.

If you've parked near the road on the east side, paddle to the

OPPOSITE: The view from the Kirkstile Inn.

BELOW: Crummock Water from the shore near Lanthwaite Woods.

35 LAKE DISTRICT 175

CLOCKWISE FROM TOP LEFT: Pretty Lake District scenery near Buttermere; paddling on Buttermere; the wonderful Kirkstile Inn, with great food and character.

north shore and leave your kayak/SUP there to walk through the woods to the Kirkstile, or park here at The National Trust's Lanthwaite Wood's car park, between the two.

▸ Details

Explore The Lakes (*explorethelakes.co.uk*) offers mobile paddleboard hire, delivering to the Crummock Water area. See the Paddle UK website (*gopaddling.info/lakes/crummock-water*) for map and info; you need a day permit for the lake, not included in the Paddle UK licence, available from the car park and the Pay By Phone app (*nationaltrust.org.uk/visit/lake-district/buttermere-valley/boating-and-fishing-in-the-buttermere-valley*).

▸ Make a weekend of it

Stay in the glorious Kirkstile Inn (*kirkstile.com*), which has done up its rooms in contemporary style in recent years, or one of dozens of nearby cottages; there are dozens of operators offering cosy hideaways in the area. Don't miss a peek at lovely Loweswater church.

▸ Alternative route

The next lake along to the north, Loweswater, has no lakeside boozer, but is quiet and very beautiful, and a short walk from the Kirkstile Inn. It's a small lake, possible to circuit within an hour or so. Approach on the south side, a bit of a walk of 15 minutes or so from the National Trust's small Maggie's Bridge car park. Get in near the National Trust's shoreside Holme Wood Bothy, which you can hire as basic accommodation, sleeping six – a bothy in the true sense of the word, not the glamping variety (*nationaltrust.org.uk/holidays/lake-district/holme-wood-bothy*). Buy a licence to paddle here from the carparks in Buttermere, Crummock or the Pay By Phone App (*nationaltrust.org.uk/visit/lake-district/buttermere-valley/boating-and-fishing-in-the-buttermere-valley*) and (*gopaddling.info/lakes/loweswater*). I enjoyed circuiting the lake by the shore, playing wobble board (where two of you stand on your paddleboards and wrestle, trying to knock the other off), and making tea in a Kelly Kettle on the pebbles afterwards. It's a lake for long leisurely enjoyment, often deserted even in summer, though popular with wild swimmers – mind their heads.

Cumbria

36 Lake District: Bassenthwaite Lake

- 1.5km (1 mile) flexible
- Scenic, quiet, historic
- Lake
- Out and back
- Licence needed

How many lakes are there in the Lake District? Only one, actually – Bassenthwaite Lake. All the others are meres and waters, if you go by their names.

Not exactly isolated, but not too busy with tourists either, Bassenthwaite is a lake with just enough going on to keep it interesting. A sailing club at the north end, a couple of hotels and cafes, the Mirehouse and Gardens manor house (*mirehouse.com*), open to visitors in the south, and along the western edge, the A66, bringing an audible rumble to an otherwise jaw-dropping scene. Paddle out though, and all sounds of human life drop away. The volume is turned up on nature's playlist instead – bird calls, sploshing fish and the whistling wind. Then you can enjoy this characterful lake, with the sight of mighty Skiddaw, one of the highest Cumbrian mountains at 931m (3,054ft), rearing to the east.

Dodd Wood, fringing the peak's base, was famously where a breeding pair of ospreys returned in 2001, after no osprey nests had been recorded in the Lakes in 150 years (*visitcumbria.com/kes/osprey-watch*). The population is thriving, and when they

BELOW: Paddleboarders out and about on Bassenthwaite Lake.

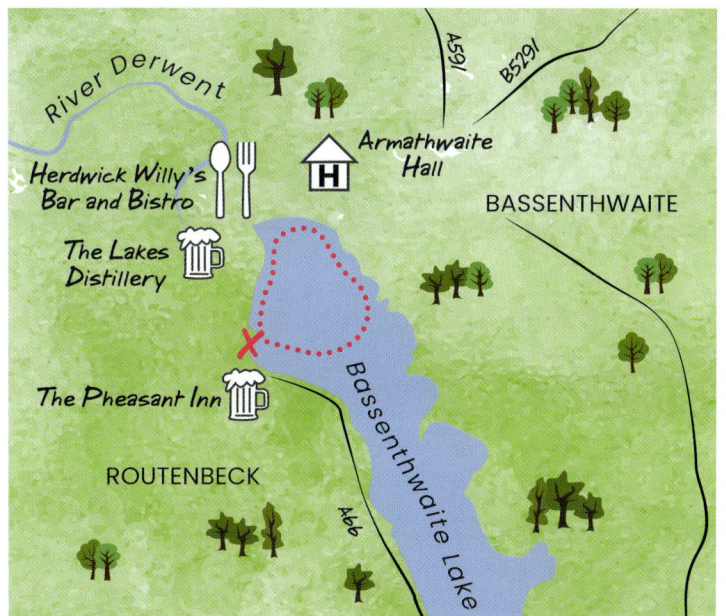

come over from West Africa to breed between April and September, you may see these beauties circling, swooping and fishing. Look out too for warblers, reed buntings, geese and meadow pipits; though as always, paddlers should be mindful and not get close.

Such abundant wildlife has made Bassenthwaite a National Nature Reserve. Motorboats are banned, there are 'no boating' zones in the south, and it's forbidden to land at all along much of the southern shoreline. You will have to admire millennia-old St Bega's Church from the water, or return on foot through the Mirehouse grounds later. Paddlers should enter the water via the purpose-built pontoon and slipway at Peel Wyke, a couple of minutes off the A66, with parking along the road.

The wind can come on quite strong, so stick to the periphery. A full loop is about 13 or 14km (8 or 9 miles), so you might prefer to go up and down the eastern shore.

As I paddle here, I relive memories of a primary school trip in the 1980s, when my class wrote poetry on the misty shores at dawn (to be performed to an Enya backing track in assembly back home). Bassenthwaite then seemed the most mystical place on earth – maybe with just the right amount of mist it will to you, too.

The lake empties into the River Derwent at the north end (it

BELOW: The Pheasant Inn near Bassenthwaite (photo: The Pheasant Inn).

TOP TO BOTTOM: The Pheasant Inn near Bassenthwaite; Armathwaite Hall from the lake; the cosy bar inside The Pheasant.

pours in at the south), where it's fast flowing and can take you by surprise, so paddle hard across as it tumbles out beneath you and under Ouse Bridge. Just before the bridge is a nice little beach sheltered by trees. The beaches on the other side are privately owned by **Armathwaite Hall**, a luxury hotel visible from the water. You are allowed to pull in if you're heading up for a drink in the bar, on the condition you don't drip all over it – they request you sit outside if you're wet.

Other options at this end are **Herdwick Willy's Bar and Bistro** at the Herdwick Croft campsite and **The Lakes Distillery** a few minutes' walk inland. The distillery has a bistro in what was once a Victorian farmstead's cattle barn, plus offers tours and tastings of its fabulous vodkas (the toffee is delicious), gins and whiskies.

Finish back on dry land at Peel Wyke, from where it's a hop, skip and a squelch to the 17th-century **Pheasant Inn**, an old-fashioned charmer with lovely gardens. As well as a larger bar, there's a very special tiny darkened nook that's the snuggest of snugs, with red lacquered ceilings and walls, heavy dark wood furniture, and framed vintage photos and maps.

▶ Details

Paddling on Bassenthwaite requires a permit, available online on the tourist board website (*lakedistrict.gov.uk/visiting/things-to-do/water/bassenthwaite-permits/boat-permits*). See a map at (*lakedistrict.gov.uk/__data/assets/pdf_file/0017/112805/Bassenthwaite-map.pdf*). For more route details see the Paddle UK website (*gopaddling.info/lakes/bassenthwaite-lake*). Explore The Lakes (*explorethelakes.co.uk*) offers mobile paddleboard hire. See (*lakesdistillery.com*).

▶ Make a weekend of it

It's a real treat to stay in one of the smart rooms at the Pheasant Inn (*inncollectiongroup.com/pheasant-inn*), where a hearty Cumbrian breakfast is included. Luxury hotel Armathwaite Hall (*armathwaite-hall.com*) is set in 400 acres of deer park and woodland that runs down to the waterside. It may cost an arm and a leg, but when yours are aching, that spa is going to feel good. Herdwick Croft Holiday Park's (*herdwickcroft.co.uk*) camping pitches, cottages, or wooden cabins and lodges with hot tubs are another option.

BELOW: The wooded hills above Bassenthwaite.

Cumbria

37 Lake District: Ullswater

- 4.8km (3 miles)
- Mountains, glamour, scenery
- Lake
- Out and back
- No licence needed

As the Lake District's second biggest lake, shaped like an upside-down question mark, Ullswater has a bounty of curves and corners to explore, though it's also one of the busiest. This can mean having to dodge dinghies, wakeboarders and the famous paddlesteamers, which criss-cross between several stops. Here's where paddlers can get creative: use the steamers for return routes, or to miss sections you don't fancy.

Since it opened in 2017 on Ullswater's north-west shore, Another Place has gained a reputation as the ultimate contemporary luxury hotel in the Lake District – a refutation to the idea that Cumbria's accommodation is all chintz or muddy boots. It's the sister hotel to Cornwall's famous style-and-surfing hotel Watergate Bay, so it's trendy, sexy and cool.

But don't write it off even if you're a damp, scruffy paddler just after a cuppa or half an ale on the shore. Yes, there may be floor-to-ceiling glass in the posh indoor pool, designer shepherd's huts with copper tubs in the gardens, elegant dining rooms with indigo wood panelling, and monochrome zigzag tiled floors. But it's also totally tailored to outdoorsy types, too, and all are welcome. If you're paddling over yourself, be sure to stop for the

BELOW: Paddleboarders on Ullswater, one of the largest lakes in the Lake District (photo: Another Place).

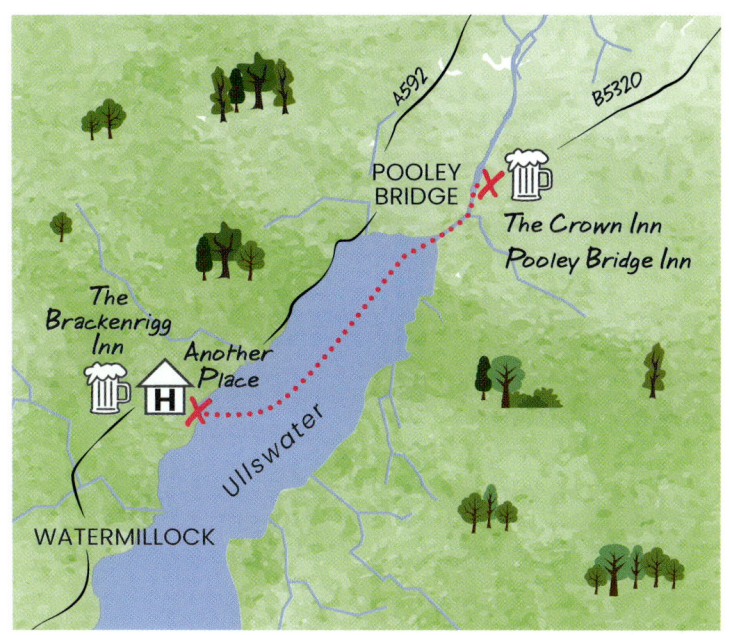

hotel's glamorous **Glasshouse** garden bar. Housed in a Victorian-style greenhouse, it is the closest of the hotel's bars and restaurants to the water, with a pontoon bearing a sign to welcome boaters. An outdoor seating area near the vegetable patch and herb garden is a gorgeous place to relax. The Glasshouse interior is strung with lights, pot plants line the window sills, and a wood-fired pizza oven steams up the glass. Come for coffee, beer or a negroni, made with Lakes Distillery spirits.

Even if you're not staying at the hotel, you can make use of its watersports centre, the Sheep Shed, which offers guided wild swimming, and kayak and paddleboard hire.

From Another Place, there's an enjoyable 2.4km (1.5 miles) paddle heading north to Pooley Bridge, a touristy enclave with pubs and cafes. As you approach the bridge from the south, the flow from the incoming River Eamont is strong but shallow. I found it easier to get out and wade rather than paddle against the current. You immediately come upon a line of waterside venues comprising Granny Dowbekins tearoom (grannydowbekins.co.uk), which has been serving scones since 1904; the **Secret Garden** bar and restaurant, and the pub you are heading for, **The Crown Inn**. It's a bold, jazzed-up number with a waterside beer garden and pontoon. The cheap and cheerful **Pooley Bridge Inn** is just slightly

BELOW: Ullswater has lots of activities to try (photo: Another Place).

37 LAKE DISTRICT 183

CLOCKWISE FROM TOP: Lunch at the Brackenrigg Inn; Ullswater from above; approaching The Crown Inn on the River Eamont; dining at Another Place (photo: Another Place).

inland, with a big green beer garden.

All are rather touristy and lack character, but sitting at a bench next to my kayak at The Crown in summer, I enjoyed watching busy river life unfold – children fishing on the opposite shore, dogs rushing into the water, kayakers pulling in for a pint of Thwaites ale.

All seemed well with the world. To return, you might make use of the steamer as there's a stop at Pooley Bridge. Take it back down to Glenridding at the other end, for example.

❱ Details

Hire kayaks, rafted canoes and paddleboards from Another Place's watersports centre (*another.place/active*). Download a detailed map of the Ullswater Canoe Trail, which shows places to stop, access to the water and things to see, created by conservation charity Eden Rivers Trust (*edenriverstrust.org.uk/things-to-do/ullswater-canoe-trail*). Pooley Bridge's Park Foot campsite has parking and launching for a small fee. There are several other hire places around the lake, see (*ullswaterpaddleboarding.co.uk*), (*ullswateroutdooradventures.co.uk*) and (*alfrescoadventures.co.uk*). No licence needed. For a map, see (*lakedistrict.gov.uk/__data/assets/pdf_file/0022/106870/Ullswater-map.pdf*). For pubs, see (*secretgardenrestaurant.co.uk*), (*crownpooleybridge.co.uk*) and (*pooleybridgeinn.co.uk*).

❱ Make a weekend of it

Another Place (*another.place*) is a smashing hotel, frequently voted one of the UK's best and most original, with mega stylish rooms as well as super-smart shepherd's huts (these shepherds would have designer sandals and silver crooks) and a treehouse in neatly manicured grounds. Its second venue on the lake, Brackenridge Inn (*another.place/the-brackenrigg-inn*) is a smaller pub, just as cool, with lake views, and a microbrewery. The Crown Inn (*crownpooleybridge.co.uk*) has decent rooms with glossy bathrooms in jewel colours, tartan blankets, exposed brick and raw wood headboards.

❱ Alternative routes

At the Glenridding end, the **Inn On The Lake** (*lakedistricthotels.net/innonthelake/eat-and-drink*) is a four star hotel by the water, with a bright and modern Ramblers Bar among its restaurants.

BELOW: You could spend days paddling Ullswater.

More great paddles in the Lake District

Only 12 Lake District lakes can be paddled. Of these 12, a few have banned SUPs, so only canoes and kayaks are allowed on Ennerdale Water, Rydal Water and Thirlmere Reservoir (*lakedistrict.gov.uk/visiting/things-to-do/water/access-to-the-lakes*). But there are the rivers too, which provide excellent paddling opportunities, as well as the Cumbrian coast.

WINDERMERE

A popular route on Windermere, the national park's biggest lake, is to get in at the Fell Foot car park at the southern end, then head along the River Leven to Newby Bridge and back, a 5.6km (3.5 mile) round trip. Before returning, call in at the Swan Hotel (*swanhotel.com*) for a drink in its pubby **Swan Inn**, with mossy green walls and floral chairs and wallpaper. See the national park website (*lakedistrict.gov.uk*) for maps, info and routes. Several operators rent crafts and offer lessons on the lake, see (*windermerecanoekayak.com*) and (*graythwaiteadventure.co.uk*). The lake is tragically having its ecosystem destroyed by sewage infiltration, but that doesn't mean paddlers should avoid it. Just be careful about where you swim and splash. See the brilliant Save Windermere (*savewindermere.com*) to get involved or donate to the conservation campaign, and show the government and water companies how much we value our bodies of water for recreation and relaxation. It also has a map of worst affected spots.

RIGHT: The Swan Inn near Windermere (photo: The Swan Inn).

BUTTERMERE TO THE SEA ON THE RIVER COCKER AND RIVER DERWENT

It's possible to do an expedition from Buttermere to the coast, a 22-mile (36km) route that goes along the lake and into Crummock Water, then onto the River Cocker, following it to the confluence with the River Derwent at Cockermouth. The operator iGuide Adventure (*iguideadventure.com*), sells this as a two-day camping and canoeing trip via Wild Plans (*wildplans.com*), with the option of staying in a pub or hotel en route instead, and sometimes hoisting sails to speed the canoes. You can take a break in lively Cockermouth, a town full of pubs, before continuing to Workington and the coast.

RYDAL WATER AND RIVER ROTHAY TO THE BADGER BAR

Kayaks and canoes, but not paddleboards, are currently allowed on Rydal Water, where the River Rother leads out from its eastern edge to one of the quirkiest pub experiences imaginable. We're talking badgers. Yep, at the Glen Rothay Hotel (*theglenrothay.co.uk*), the **Badger Bar** draws punters keen not just to sip the real local ales on offer, but to wait with baited breath in the gardens to watch the badgers who roll up after dark to be fed. For the best chance of seeing them, including cute cubs, come between April and October. You'll relish the quaint character of the 17th-century pub too, with its open fires, beer gardens and loos built into the rockface.

RIVER ESK TO RAVENGLASS AND THE RATTY ARMS

A fun there-and-back of whatever length you choose is a run with the tide up the River Esk from Ravenglass. My pal, *Times* travel writer, Sean Newsom called it 'the loveliest of all waterside settlements in Cumbria'. The town is linked to the magnificent Eskdale Valley by the famous steam line, the Ravenglass and Eskdale Railway (*ravenglass-railway.co.uk*). Incidentally, the railway has its own pub on the platform, the **Ratty Arms**, where after your paddle it's fun to sit and watch the trains. There are a few other pubs in Ravenglass. You can also paddle to the town along the River Irt, putting in at Holm Bridge. West Lakes Adventure runs trips on this route (*westlakesadventure.co.uk/activities/kayaking*).

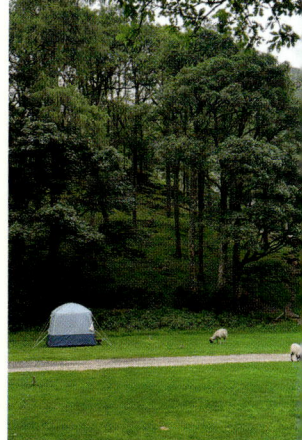

ABOVE: Camping near the River Derwent.

MORE GREAT PADDLES IN THE LAKE DISTRICT   187

ABOVE: A pebble beach on the River Derwent, Cumbria.

WASTWATER AND THE WASDALE HEAD INN

With the stark and foreboding drama of a Greenlandic fjord, Wastwater, in the west of the National Park, is scarily deep – 80m (260ft) in parts – and 4.8km (3 miles) long, flanked on the east side by sheer scree. Yet, turn on the sunshine and its little sandy coves can feel positively Mediterranean. There's nowhere like it, but it's somewhere you need to be very careful paddling and come off-season, if you can. The local authorities are trying to discourage paddling here due to past incidents and overcrowding on the minor road that runs along the west side – make sure you park well off the road so emergency vehicles can get through (see advice at (*adventuresmart.uk*)). There are grassy places to park if you get there early. Up the northern end, it's a 1.6km (1 mile) walk (or drive) from the water to the **Wasdale Head Inn** (*wasdale.com*). It's a classic higgledy-piggledy mountaineers' pub that's been welcoming travellers – including Samuel Taylor Coleridge and Charles Dickens – for two centuries. Bedrooms are basic. A National Trust campsite nearby has heated camping pods and glamping (*nationaltrust.org.uk/holidays/lake-district/wasdale-campsite*).

OTHER OPTIONS

Still need more? Try Grasmere, a small and very pretty lake, quite sheltered so good for a wild and windy day. The honeypot village is famed for its gingerbread but has a few pubs too. Derwentwater is a dramatic stunner, while the River Eden is popular for whitewater.

More great paddles in the Northwest

SALFORD QUAYS

Home to The Lowry theatre and arts venue, as well as creative and tech hub MediaCity, Salford Quays has risen from a grimy past to become a thriving part of Greater Manchester, with snazzy bars and restaurants near the water. Salford Watersports (*salfordwatersports.com*) hires out SUPs, giant SUPs and kayaks, and offers beginners' lessons, as well as open water swimming sessions. In winter it runs moonlit paddles, which is a great warm up for a cosy pub session at the **Dockyard** (*dockyard.pub/media-city*), a self-proclaimed 'rustic ale house'. If you're after somewhere dark and decadent where the cocktail menu comes in categories, **The Alchemist** (*thealchemistbars.com/venues/mediacity-uk-manchester*) has a terrace over the water.

LANCASTER CANAL

Sometimes it's worth hunting out the lesser-known spots. In the little village of Bilsbarrow in Lancashire, north of Preston, Countryside Canoes (*countrysidecanoes.co.uk*) hires out Canadian-style canoes by the day from a spot opposite the **Roe Buck** pub (*chefandbrewer.com/pubs/lancashire/roebuck*). Go for a gentle meander through an area of thatched cottages, fields and farms, then return for a pie. For a farther foray, carry on to two other waterside pubs in Guys Thatched Hamlet, a village-cum-attraction that is home to a cricket ground and lodge accommodation. There's a quaint white pub, **Owd Nells** (*guysthatchedhamlet.co.uk/explore-the-hamlet/owd-nells-canalside-tavern*), or try the **White Bull** (no website), small and simple with a canalside garden.

BELOW: The Royal Albert Docks, Liverpool (photo: iStock).

ABOVE: The aqueduct carrying the Lancaster Canal over the River Lune (photo: iStock).

RIVER MERSEY TO SALE

On a calm, typically canal-flat section of the Mersey, Venture Out Activity Centre (*venture-out.co.uk/mersey-metrolink*) in Burnage runs a 3.5 hour, one way kayak trip (guided or self-led) of about 11km (7 miles) to the **Jackson's Boat pub** (*jacksonsboatsale.co.uk*) in Sale, for pizzas, pub grub and its own Jackson's Boat Ale. The ale is brewed by nearby Cheshire's Beartown brewery in my hometown of Congleton, which legendarily sold its communal town Bible to buy a bear in in the 17th century. There's a pay and display car park near the pub for independent paddlers and the Metrolink tram links the locations.

LIVERPOOL'S ROYAL ALBERT DOCKS

The heart of global trade in the 19th century, Liverpool's Royal Albert Docks are the northwest's most visited site, a World Heritage site of grand red-brick buildings. Attractions from the Beatles Story to the Tate Liverpool (*albertdock.com*) draw the crowds, but why not rent kayaks or SUPs from the Liverpool Watersports Centre (*wtm360.co.uk/sales/liverpool-watersport-centre*) to paddle around this historic zone and admire it from the water. Those with their own gear can buy a pass to launch here too, and there are lessons available and open water swimming. For the perfect post-paddle pub stop, **The Pumphouse** (*greeneking.co.uk/pubs/merseyside/pump-house*), which first supplied power to the docks in 1870, occupies a red-brick building with a towering chimney in the World Heritage Site, with a big stone terrace overlooking the water.

RIGHT: Liverpool's Royal Albert Docks (photo: iStock).

Scotland

Scotland

38 River Tweed: Peebles to Innerleithen

- 11 to 48km (7 to 30 miles)
- Historical, hills, peaceful
- River
- One way
- No licence needed

Famous as one of Scotland's most productive salmon fishing rivers foremostly, the Tweed has possibly been overlooked for other pursuits. Paddlers will love the easy floating between the hills of the Border country, with plenty of stop-offs to top up on vittles en route.

To promote this 145km (90 mile) river for more varied forms of fun, in 2024, the Tweed Valley Canoe Trail was created as the first official canoe route in southern Scotland. Running for around 50km (30 miles), it links landmarks such as Neidpath Castle and Sir Walter Scott's home, Abbotsford, as it winds from Stobo in the east to Tweedbank.

The route could be tackled by strong paddlers in one day

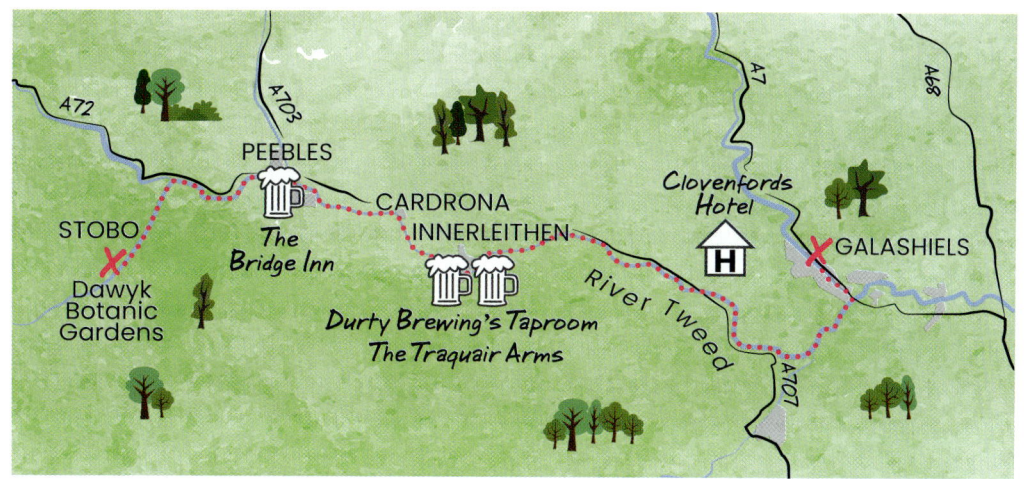

(though you'd have to forgo the tea breaks and pub stops) or it can be bitten off in chunks. The tourist board creators say the waymarked route falls into six sections, each between 3.2 to 13km (2 to 8 miles). The official bumf provides paddler-friendly suggestions of what to see and do on the way (including pub stops).

Stobo to Peebles is an easy run of 11km (7 miles), which takes about three hours. It starts near Dawyk Botanic Garden, a flower-filled park run by the Royal Botanic Garden of Edinburgh that you may want to visit first. From there, it passes Lyne Station, which offers a rest stop, followed by a disused viaduct and the fortified medieval tower of Neidpath Castle. There are some popular swimming spots before Peebles. At the town, pause by Cuddy Bridge to check the conditions of the weir, which can be tackled (stay to the left of the island), or portaged if you exit at the bridge. End at Peebles' Kingsmeadows car park and nip to the community-focused and simple **The Bridge Inn**.

Section two of the route is 6.4km (4 miles) through wooded hills to Cardrona, then an attractive 4.8km (3 miles) to the lively town of Innerleithen, home to **Durty Brewing's Taproom**. Not only does it make great beers but the company also runs outdoor events such as triathlons, fell runs and mountain bike downhillers. **The Traquair Arms** is a characterful pub in the same town, a 200-year old coaching inn with a beer garden. Innerleithen is a good place to end or stay, but if you make it as far as Galashiels there's decent pub grub at the **Clovenfords Hotel**.

OPPOSITE: The Bridge Inn, Peebles, on the River Tweed (photo: Visit Scotland).

CLOCKWISE FROM BELOW: The River Tweed on a summer's day (photo: Visit Scotland); a sign on the banks; Neidpath Castle from the river (photo: iStock).

194 SCOTLAND

❱ Details

For a map of the Tweed Valley Canoe Trail with more information, see (gotweedvalley.co.uk/explore-tweed-valley-canoe-trail and gopaddling.info/rivers/river-tweed). Hire canoes or kayaks and arrange multi-day trips with Biggar Adventure (biggaradventure.co.uk); or hire from Kayak & SUP Hire Scottish Borders (scotlandstartshere.com), which can deliver kayaks and SUPs. Sessions on the River Tweed and sea kayaking on the Tweed Estuary can be booked with Active 4 Season (active4seasons.co.uk/sea-kayaking-in-northumberland). Paddlers are encouraged to do the trip between April and September to avoid the October/November fishing season. Borders Buses run along the route for those needing to return to a hotel or start point by road. For pubs see, (thebridgeinnpeebles.co.uk), (durtybrewing.com/the-tap-room), (traquairarmshotel.co.uk) and (theclovenfordshotel.co.uk).

❱ Make a weekend of it

Just 1.6km (1 mile) from Peebles, Neidpath Castle (neidpathcastle.com), which you'd pass as you paddle, has chambers and cottages to stay in, some with outdoor wood-fired baths. Or in Peebles try The Park (parkpeebles.co.uk) a stylish 25-room boutique hotel that reflects the town's textile-making heritage in its decor. Cardrona has the Macdonald Cardrona hotel and spa (macdonaldhotels.co.uk/cardrona); Traquair Arms has 16 stylish rooms and six cottages.

BELOW: The River Tweed rolling through Peebles (photo: iStock).

Scotland

39 Argyll: Loch Sween and Tayvallich

- 3.2 to 6.4km (2 to 4 miles)
- Nature, beauty, wildlife
- Sea loch
- Out and back
- No licence needed

Loch Sween is a staggering sea loch where otters and seals play and where once the rulers of the Gaelic kingdom sailed their ships. On its shores is the vibrant community village of Tayvallich, home to the excellent **Tayvallich Inn**. Situated on the edge of the west coast's fingers of water near Lochgilphead, the pub is at the heart of a tiny community. Its special atmosphere is perfect on a breezy, sunny day but also cosy on a wild autumn one (or even a wild summer's one; this is Scotland after all). Established three decades ago, the pub has long been a favourite of sailors, and more recently a must-paddle pub for sea kayakers. Come on your own adventures, or book a guided escapade, such as one that departs right outside the pub, with Wild Argyll.

Here I met guide Will Self (a different one to the author) to set out with two best girlfriends on a crisp cold December day, starting from outside the pub (but leaving the drinking until afterwards, of course). The fact we were going sea kayaking had scared my friends who were concerned about big waves, but it was calm as could be, a mere ticklish ripple under our kayaks as we headed out from the protected Tayvallich Bay and into Loch Sween. Within minutes Will pointed out curlews and shags. We were aiming, like children in a storybook, for the Fairy Islands, on which we paused to munch a snack and warm our hands, slipping over mussel-clung rocks to find a spot to perch and throw our gazes seawards. Far on the horizon, an island seemed to hover above the water, like a floating Howl's Moving Castle of rock. Fata morgana, an optical illusion or mirage, explained Will.

A millennia and a half ago, the rulers of the Gaelic Kingdom, Dal Riata, would have witnessed the same and surely must have read something spiritual into the sight. This area of the north-west Scottish coast was once the very centre of that 5th-century civilisation, which stretched around the coastlines of the north of Ireland and Scotland's west coast. The protected sea lochs were ideal for fishing. The routes in and out of the lochs, and throughout their coastal, seafaring kingdom were the 'sea roads'. Kilmartin Glen, close by to the north, was their place of governance, worship and ritual, where the fort of Dunadd was the seat of Dal Raita. There are neolithic stone circles and rare rock art there. All this was utterly transporting to think about while paddling on an ice-bitten misty day. Ancient cultures felt enticingly tangible.

Whether the ancient Gaels slurped Cullen skink and gorged on plates of fresh prawns, we can only guess. But it's unlikely they could be quite so delicious as those served at the pub. Check

OPPOSITE: Loch Sween on Scotland's beautiful west coast (photo: iStock).

CLOCKWISE FROM TOP LEFT: The Tayvallich Inn; sea kayaking on Loch Sween (photo: Anne Batchelor); the shore by Tayvallich (photo: Anne Batchelor).

timings ahead (it's usually closed for some of the winter) and be sure to order a crisp pint of local brewer Fyne Ale's Avalanche beer to take your time over while you appreciate that astonishingly beautiful bay view.

❱ Details

Book a sea kayak tour from Tayvallich with Wild Argyll (*explorewildargyll.com*). For information about paddling in the area see regional websites (*visitbute.com/active/kayaking & paddleboarding*) and (*paddle-argyll.co.uk*). For the pub, see (*tayvallichinn.com*). The 150km (93 miles) Sea Kayak Argyll Trail along the coast would make a wonderful adventure, and can be divided into eight sections.

❱ Make a weekend of it

There are other options around but for a special treat, hire Kilmartin Castle (*kilmartincastle.com*), arguably Scotland's coolest castle, a 16th-century holiday rental of spiral staircases and turrets, sleeping 10 in rooms with thick stone walls and edgy, humorous artwork. You can hire private chefs to cook for you over fire and feast in the vaulted cellar or Victorian-style greenhouse. There's a wild swimming pond outside and nearby, the ancient ruins, stone circles and rock art of the Gaelic kingdom that once ruled the region, up and down the Scottish and Irish coasts.

BELOW: Loch Sween on a misty day (photo: iStock).

Scotland

40 Knoydart Peninsula and The Old Forge Inn

- 1.6 to 22.5km (1 to 14 miles)
- Remote, beauty, nature
- Sea
- Out and back
- No licence needed

The Old Forge Inn has had some times. About 15 years ago the pub – often referred to as the most remote in mainland Britain – was infamous for the spontaneous jamming sessions that would break out when the night wore on and the whisky flowed. Local folk and visitors too, if they were lucky, would be moved to take down the musical instruments hanging on the walls and burst into tune. The best nights could end up with 20 musicians or more crammed around the tiny tables, the craic going wild and carrying on late into the night. It sounded like the best party in the land, all the more so for the degree of difficulty it took to reach it, and for the ridiculous beauty of the surrounding landscapes. The Knoydart peninsula is a rocky, heathery and mountainous hunk of the west coast, cut off from civilisation, jutting out between three deep sea lochs, with no road access, and the one small village of Inverie.

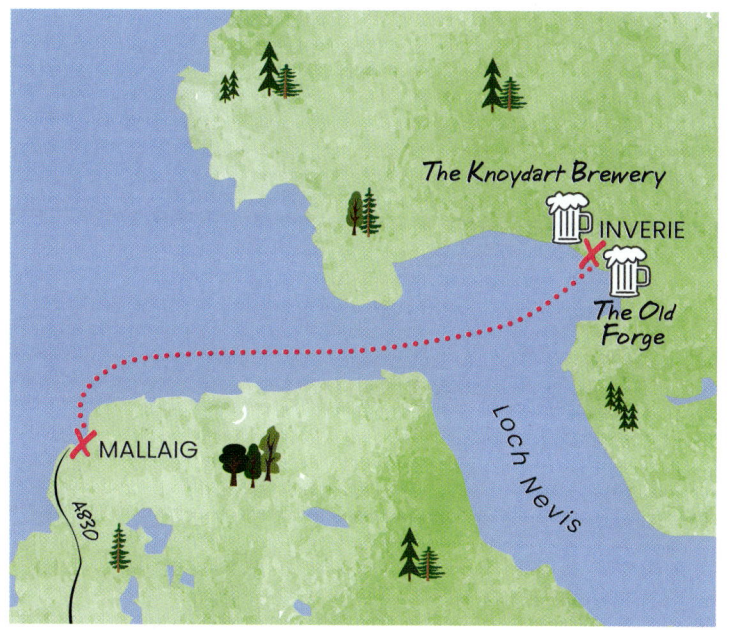

Then there was a period when things went off the boil; a new landlord was running things not quite to everyone's liking, and the pub's reputation as a legendary venue was mired. Spontaneous music sessions dwindled, many locals stopped going – this despite it being the only pub in a community of some 120 or so souls, with the nearest alternatives hours away across the water. Just when it seemed it would never be the place it once was, the Knoydart community stepped in and bought it for themselves. In 2022, the Old Forge was relaunched as a community-owned venture. Anyone who had ever been must've fist-pumped at this happy-ending tale of redemption.

It was a move that mimicked one made two decades prior, when the local community also bought out the land-owning Knoydart Estate, creating the Knoydart Foundation to provide low income housing and renewable energy to those living around Inverie Bay.

Now the Old Forge is thriving again, the old magic recaptured, and the interior improved under the care of The Old Forge Benefit Society. And the folk music plays loud and late once more.

The question remains, how will you get there? Knoydart is hemmed by deep wild sea lochs where seals play and white-tailed eagles soar: Loch Nevis on the south side, Loch Hourn to the

OPPOSITE: The rugged Knoydart Peninsula (photo: iStock).

BELOW: Many visitors cross by boat from Mallaig (photo: iStock).

ABOVE: The Sound of Sleat (photo: iStock).

north, and the Sound of Sleat to the west. Mountains behind separate it from inland Scotland.

One way is to make the day's hike from Kinlochhourn (a taxi ride from Fort William), or take one of the other hiking paths that lead there (Glenfinnan or Glen Dessary are alternative start points). Many arrive on the Knoydart Western Isles Ferry from Mallaig, a small ex-fishing boat which also connects to Tarbert in Loch Nevis. Private RIB charters can be booked too, but you could also paddle to it.

The most direct route, from Mallaig, is some 11.2km (7 miles) – quite strenuous and splashy ones. Several operators offer touring trips of a few days in the area, typically including wild camping and hillwalking.

Far easier is to take the ferry then hire a sit-on-top kayak locally, with Love Knoydart and head out for a short kilometre (half a mile) between the glowering grey rocks to the pale sands of Long Beach, or explore up the River Inverie as far as you like.

The pub pontoon has space for six boats, or it's easy to pull up on the beaches. The simple white, one-story building has barely changed since the 1770s. It was a cottage first, then a smiddy's smelting forge and a workers' club, before turning into a pub.

The **Knoydart Brewery**, occupying the old deconsecrated Roman Catholic chapel of St Agnes, supplies the house ales (its tagline is: 'wilderness in a bottle'). Knoydart venison from the local deer estate is a menu must, along with Cullen skink or battered Mallaig haddock.

Other great little businesses here include the stalwart Knoydart Pottery and Tea Room, and Knoydart Coffee, a small batch artisan roaster. If you're looking for fine dining, The Lookout bistro has an outdoor deck and views to Loch Nevis.

If you're going somewhere so remote, you really must stay. A few days should do it. On my last trip, I rambled the banks, beaches and forests around the shore, watching sea otters playing in the shallows near our holiday cabin and the stars at night, gorging on seafood and pints in the pub in between. Holiday perfection.

▶ Details

For information about Knoydart, getting there, around, where to stay and what to do, see (*visitknoydart.co.uk*). The Old Forge Inn (*theoldforge.co.uk*) keeps summer hours from April to October, so check times before visiting, also see (*knoydartbrewery.co.uk*) and (*loveknoydart.co.uk*). Several adventure operators run sea kayak expeditions to Knoydart. Among them, Arisaig Sea Kayak Centre (*arisaigseakayakcentre.co.uk*) can tailor-make day and multi-day trips; Unexplored Scotland (*unexplored.scot*) offers longer walking and kayaking holidays, as does Active Outdoor Pursuits (*activeoutdoorpursuits.com*). For restaurant, see (*thegatheringknoydart.co.uk*).

▶ Make a weekend of it

There are multiple accommodation options on the peninsula. Cute cabins called Wee Hooses (*knoydart.org/wee-hooses*) add colour to the foot of the Black Hills; there's the Bunkhouse, which does what it says on the tin; and camping with views across the bay to the Isle of Rum (*knoydart.org/knoydart-bunkhouse*). The Gathering (*thegatheringknoydart.co.uk/bed-breakfast-knoydart*) has B&B rooms, self-catering and a hot tub, or go luxury at Knoydart Hide (*knoydarthide.co.uk*) and Knoydart House's (*knoydarthouse.co.uk*) posh, self-catered pads.

BELOW: The village of Inverie on the Knoydart Peninsula (photo: iStock).

Scotland

41 The Highlands: Wester Ross and the Applecross Inn

- 3.2 to 32km (2 to 20 miles)
- Beauty, wild, remote
- Sea
- Out and back
- No licence needed

Up in the north-west Highlands of Scotland in Wester Ross, the gobsmackingly gorgeous Applecross peninsula juts into the Inner Sound, between the mountains of the mainland and Skye to the west. For anyone driving, cycling, hiking or paddling the west coast, it's an absolute must – the **Applecross Inn** is so renowned I've seen diners drop in by helicopter for a slap-up seafood lunch.

And what a lunch! The hand-dived scallops are as succulent as a mermaid's snog, served here with bacon and pea puree. The half dozen local oysters will be the ones you compare all other oysters to afterwards. The Applecross Bay prawns in hot garlic butter is a sticky messy feast, and dressed local crab or battered monkfish are done to perfection. These are dishes people come from far and wide for.

During the busiest, warmer months from April until October, there's outdoor dining in the beer garden opposite the simple-looking white inn, where you can let your gaze fall across the sun-sparkled water to the islands of Raasay and Skye. If you come by road, you'll need to relax and come down off the journey once you get there. The inn lies on a ribboning, steep road they have used to shoot *Top Gear*, and which hosts annual cycle races. Dramatic yes, nerve-jangling... also yes. But perhaps, you clever thing, you'll have come by sea, paddling around these beautiful bays all day and ending here to immerse yourself in sheer natural beauty (and maybe a beer or two).

One of the best ways to really embed the soul into this spectacular landscape is with a sea kayaking and wild camping expedition, such as those offered by Mountain Sea Guides, based near the pub. It has half-days and taster sessions but also beginner overnight wild camping breaks where the wild can work itself into your bones. They'll kit you out with the full set up – from tents and kayaks to flares and VHF radios if you go independently. One of your group must have a BCU sea kayak training certificate to go without a guide. The paddling is thrilling: steely seas under huge empty skies; seals, otters and dolphins playing; a salt-sharp cold tinge to the air.

OPPOSITE: The Applecross Inn in Wester Ross, famed for its seafood.

CLOCKWISE FROM TOP LEFT: The Applecross peninsula juts into the Inner Sound; the dramatic route to the pub is popular with road-trippers; the high mountain scenery of Wester Ross in winter (photo: Visit Scotland).

After your adventures and back at the pub, the drinking's almost as good as the eating thanks to the inn having its own brewery, which supplies a hoppy Applecross pale ale, Sanctuary red bitter, Gold Ale IPA and a lager. The drinks list features a detailed map of Scotland marking dozens of distilleries from which the spirits, gins and whiskies hail, and a varied wine list with several champagnes (I had mentioned the helicopters). Maybe you'll want to cancel that chopper home.

▸ Details

Book expeditions and short trips in the area with operators including Mountain Sea Guides (*applecross.uk.com/msg*); and well-planned kayak holidays with Wilderness Scotland (*wildernessscotland.com*). Read about the area at (*visitapplecross.com*).

▸ Make a weekend of it

The Applecross Inn has seven simple rooms for B&B, and that second 'B' will be poached smoked haddock or local smoked salmon, black pudding sausages or the full Scottish works. More basic are the Applecross Campsite's camping huts (*visitapplecross.com*); or try the Hartfield House Hostel and Bunkhouse (*hartfieldhouse.org.uk*), which has simple white rooms of all sizes from dorms to doubles. A souped-up holiday house with hot tubs that sometimes hosts yoga retreats is Eagle Rock (*eaglerockscotland.co.uk*).

BELOW: The dramatic Applecross Peninsula.

More great paddles in Scotland

RIVER TAY TO THE OLD SHIP INN, PERTH

Known throughout the world as one of the great rivers for salmon fishing, the Tay can also be quite the catch for paddlers. It's possible to descend it almost from its source at Ben Lui, for 140km (87 miles) as it charts a dramatic course through the Highlands, flowing east to Perth on the estuary. Otters, beavers and Highland cattle may appear. There are lochs to cross, including Loch Lomond and Loch Tay, history-filled villages, Douglas fir forest and a good old pub or two at day's end. Operators run multi-day trips, typically involving wild camping and some mild whitewater sections (*activeoutdoorpursuits.com*, *northstaradventure.co.uk* and *beyondadventure.co.uk*). End in Perth at the, olde worlde and tucked away, the **Old Ship Inn** (*oldshipinnperth.co.uk*), which is the city's oldest bar, dating to 1665, with tiny wood-panelled rooms.

TIREE, INNER HEBRIDES FOR THE REEF INN

The Hawaii of the north, they call it, Tiree: huge mile-long sweep of bright white sand, curling waves that surfers dribble over, lu au and lei... well maybe not the last bit, but the rest is there. A ferry ride from Oban brings you to an incredible island of beaches, traditional blackhouses, rock art and outdoor adventuring – particularly surfing and paddlesports. Suds Surf School (*surfschoolscotland.co.uk*) has SUPs to hire, Blackhouse Watersports (*blackhouse-watersports.co.uk*) has kayaks, Wild Diamond (*wilddiamond.co.uk*) has both. Bars wise, there are the ones in the **Tiree Lodge Hotel** (*tireelodgehotel.com*) and **Scarinish Beach Hotel** (*scarinishbeachhotel.com*), the cool **Reef Inn** (*reef-tiree.com*) or relative newcomer the **Ceabhar Restaurant and Brewery** (*facebook.com/Ceabhar*). Make it over to neighbour Coll, and the only pub and restaurant on the island there is the **Coll Hotel** (*collhotel.com*), for draught beers and malt whisky.

THE STEAMBOAT, NEAR CARSETHORN, DUMFRIES

The tartan-carpeted, wood-panelled pool room of the **Steamboat Inn** (*facebook.com/TheSteamboatInn*) has a canoe hanging on

OPPOSITE: The River Tay flowing through Perth (photo: iStock).

BELOW: Enjoying the view over the River Tay (photo: iStock).

ABOVE: A lock on the Caledonian Canal near Loch Ness (photo: iStock).

BELOW: Paddling through Glasgow on the River Clyde (photo: iStock).

the wall, alongside fox heads and antlers. Outside, a grassy beer garden overlooks the Carse Gut, a channel flowing into the sea, forming a safe nook that made Danish Vikings first establish a village here. Carsethorn is still a small, peaceful coastal enclave with paddling to cliffs and empty beaches.

GREAT GLEN CANOE TRAIL: DORES INN, LOCH NESS

Scotland's best-known paddle challenge is the watery sister to the Great Glen Way footpath, crossing the country for 97km (60 miles), from Fort William to Inverness. It links the Caledonian Canal through Highlands scenery from Gairlochy, Loch Lochy, Loch Oich, and Loch Ness in 3 to 5 days. Much Better Adventures (*muchbetteradventures.com*) is one of the operators that has a five-day wild camping trip ending at Inverness. It stops off for a night out at the **Dores Inn** (*thedoresinn.co.uk*), a pretty white cottage pub with waterside garden on Loch Ness.

GLASGOW'S INN DEEP, OR GLASGOW TO EDINBURGH

Book a kayaking session to explore Glasgow from the water with Pinkston hire (*pinkston.co.uk/activities/kayaking-canoeing*), then chill at the riverside **Inn Deep** (*inndeep.com*) on the west side of the city. They offer craft beers and modern bar food, such as salt and chilli mushrooms with kimchi. Go one further and try conquering the Edinburgh to Glasgow canoe trail, connecting the Forth and Clyde Canal and the Union Canal, staying in pubs along the way for the 4- or 5-day trip. Options include the **Boathouse Hotel in Kilsyth** (*coastandcountrypubs.com/boathouse*) on the marina, the **Star and Garter Inn** in Linlithgow (*starandgarterhotel.co.uk*), and **The Bridge Inn** in Ratho (*bridgeinn.com*).

210 SCOTLAND

Wales

42 Llyn Peninsula and the Ty Coch Inn

- 3.2km (2 miles)
- Calm, coastal, scenic
- Sea
- Out and back
- No licence needed

Right beside the sandy sweep of Porthdinllaen beach near Morfa Nefyn, curling around a protected bay behind the Nefyn headland and backed by steep hills, lies the **Ty Coch Inn**. This is one of the most beautifully located pubs in Wales. It's set on the unspoilt north coast of the Llyn Peninsula, an Area of Outstanding Natural Beauty in north-west Wales that extends into the Irish Sea.

With no access by road (except for residents), the only way to reach it is by walking, about 30 minutes over a golf course, or, of course, by paddling. You know what to do.

Protected by cliffs, this body of water is typically calm and easy to paddle, clean and invigorating. Park at the National Trust's Morfa Nefyn car park on the edge of the village, 400m (1,300ft)

from the beach. From there it's about a 1.5km (1 mile) paddle to this characterful waterside pub. Alternatively you can pay to park in the golf club car park.

Once you ditch your kayak or board on the golden sands, head inside to find an old-timey, Aladdin's Cave of a pub, where Toby jugs hang above the bar, musical instruments decorate the walls and old lanterns dangle from the ceiling. Beer tables outside overlook the soft pale sands, where drinkers watch fishing boats heading into harbour. You can't book, so cross your fingers and just turn up for pints of Brooklyn lager, Wild Horse pale ales and IPAs, and simple snacks such as open prawn sandwiches or a ploughman's.

▶ Details

For car park, see (nationaltrust.org.uk/visit/wales/porthdinllaen). To rent paddleboards for a day or several, including delivery to your location anywhere on the Llyn Peninsula (or further afield for an extra fee), book through the tourist board (discoverllyn.com/paddleboard). For the pub, see (tycoch.co.uk) for the car park.

▶ Make a weekend of it

Your best bet for accommodation on the peninsula is to rent a holiday cottage such as Boom Cottage (boomcottage.co.uk), a former boathouse near Morfa Nefyn that has been smartly converted, now with a barrel sauna and outdoor hot tub, sleeping seven from about £700 a night. Plum Guide (plumguide.com) has additional stylish stays.

OPPOSITE: The misty coastline near Morfa Nefyn on the Llyn Peninsula (photo: iStock).

Wales

43 Llangollen Canal: Pontcysyllte Aqueduct

- 8km (5 miles)
- Fun, dramatic, thrilling
- Canal
- Out and back
- Licence needed

The most controversial paddleboard route in the UK?
It may well be this one — and if you didn't realise paddleboarding could be controversial, just go online and search 'paddleboarding over the Pontcysyllte aqueduct'. The mega, terrifying, 38m (125ft) high Thomas Telford-designed engineering wonder in Denbighshire features in plenty of dubious YouTube footage showing foolhardy paddlers risking their lives to cross it standing up. Do not do it.

A sheer drop, with no protective rail, lies between you and the depths or banks of the River Dee far below. Wobble and topple and your PFD won't save you. To be clear, the Canal and River Trust that operates this section of canal absolutely forbids SUPers crossing on their boards – not even going on your knees is allowed.

Paddleboarders are very welcome to cross the gaping valley

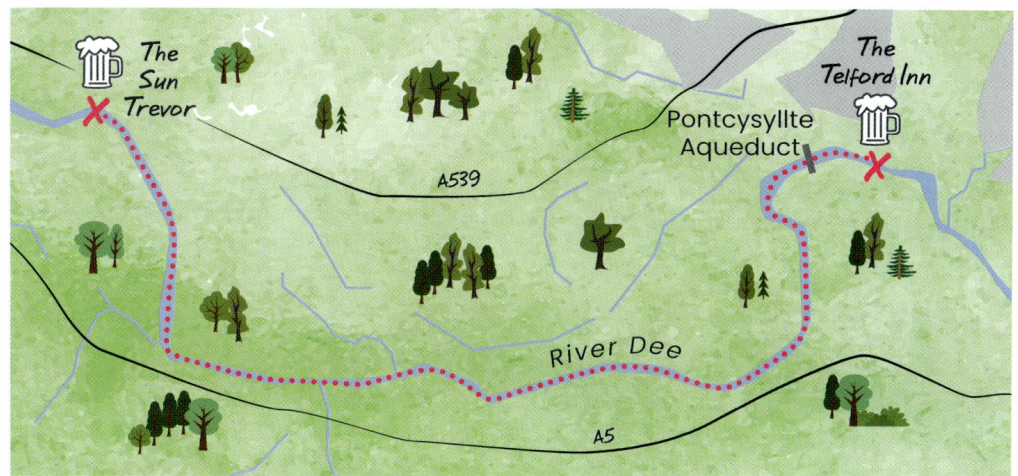

by walking beside the canal on the towpath of the 300m (895ft) long aqueduct, which does have a nice sturdy railing, pulling the board, and happily admiring the head-spinning view. Canoes and kayaks are allowed to cross on the water.

And what a view it is! The nerve-jangling drama of the drop is offset by the calming voluptuous folds of the wooded River Dee valley, curving glossy and green into the distance.

Crossing the aqueduct is just a small part of this route, and really just done for kicks and clicks (of your camera). After this most dramatic experience of your waterborne life, you'll want to soon turn around and paddle back to the Trevor Basin from whence you came. The start point is here, and those coming by car to paddle independently should park in the aqueduct car park (cheaper than those in nearby Llangollen). Nab a space right at the far end from the road entry so you won't have to carry your board/kayak too far. Then it's just a couple of minutes' walk to the Trevor Basin to get in.

This 17.7km (11 miles) of the canal comprise the Pontcysyllte Aqueduct & Canal World Heritage Site. The visitors' centre here provides insight into the manufacturing industries that necessitated the creation of the 18-arch cast iron aqueduct in 1805 to transport materials, such as iron, slate, coal and limestone.

Back at the basin coming from the aqueduct, take the left leg and paddle west along the canal for 3.5km (2.2 miles) to the Vale of Glamorgan's **The Sun Trevor**. This friendly, no-frills, down-to-earth pub occupies a glorious green spot with a beer garden,

OPPOSITE: A green and peaceful stretch of the Llangollen Canal (photo: iStock).

BELOW: Kayakers crossing the Pontcysyllte Aqueduct – paddleboarders must walk (photo: iStock).

TOP TO BOTTOM: The towpath and canal on the Pontcysyllte Aqueduct; the view of the aqueduct from the River Dee; a sunny autumnal morning on the sedate Llangollen Canal (all photos: iStock).

backed by hills. Canal, river and road all streak by in parallel below. Leave your board or kayak on the banks and scramble up for a nice glass and some simple pub food before your return. The long-standing owner, Paul Jones, is a keen paddler himself, so understands, and is amenable to people bringing paddleboards up to the garden. He fairly requests no one parks in the car park in order to paddle, even if planning to come to the pub later, as the few spaces are needed for immediate customers. It's most rewarding to arrive by water anyway, then return the same way. If you need another stop at Trevor Basin, **The Telford** pub is a bit rough and ready but will wet your whistle and sell you some crisps.

▶ Details

For information and maps, see (*canalrivertrust.org.uk*), (*gopaddling.info/canals/llangollen-canal*) and (*pontcysyllte-aqueduct.co.uk*). Hire and three-hour tours by canoe, crossing the aqueduct, are offered by Ty Nant Outdoors (*tynantoutdoors.com/activities/pontcysyllte-aqueduct-canoe-tour*); and by Bearded Men Adventure (*beardedmenadventures.com*). For pubs, see (*suntrevor.co.uk*) and (*thetelford.com*).

▶ Make a weekend of it

The pub runs holiday cottages next door, called Sun Trevor Barns (*sykescottages.co.uk*) with a hot tub, and generously offers free motorhome parking if you eat and drink there. Add some hiking to your break and follow the Offa's Dyke Path, which runs under the aqueduct.

▶ Alternative routes

For a longer option, extend the route 3.2km (2 miles) further east from the Sun Trevor to the busy little town of Llangollen, which has several pubs of its own. The riverside **Corn Mill** (*brunningandprice.co.uk/cornmill*) is a renovated old flour mill, dating back 700 years. The waterwheel turns behind the bar, and a huge deck overlooks a choppy part of the Dee. Welsh leek and potato soup and lamb faggots join Malaysian curry on the mixed menu.

Alternatively, to the west of the Trevor Basin, you can paddle further to Chirk, which also has an aqueduct that is part of the same UNESCO world heritage site, but which is a far less daunting prospect, apart from the fact it's reached through a dark tunnel.

BELOW: A canal boat on a leafy part of the canal (photo: iStock).

Wales

44 River Teifi: Cardigan and Cilgerran

- 5.6km (3.5 miles)
- Cool, dramatic, otherworldly
- River
- Out and back
- No licence needed

Flames lick the rough logs in an old stone fireplace, candles send their twitchy glow onto slate window sills, antlers decorate stone walls and warm bulbs hang from high wooden beams. Your sheepskin-laden seat is pulled up to the fire, and you nurse a cocktail with foraged botanicals, or a local ale, fresh from the cask. In this barely-converted candlelit farm building, a bar, beer taps and a fridge are the only gestures to modernity – it feels like a drinking haunt of 19th-century pastoral literature, where farmers might chew the cud over fresh cider. It's as 'cwtchy' (Welsh for 'cosy') as it gets.

A rarefied sort of cwtch you'll find here though, as the **Y Bwthyn**

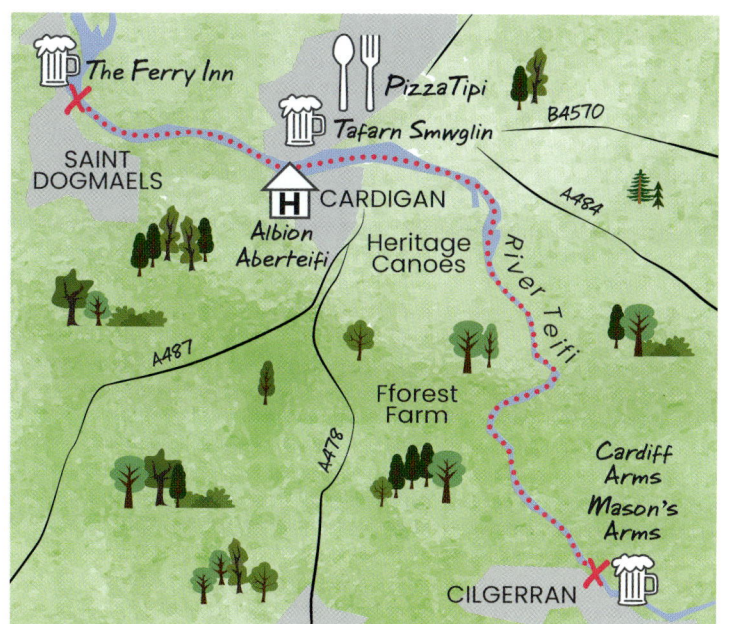

pub, tucked in a courtyard among fields and woodland, belongs to the glamping site Fforest Farm. Alas, it's open only to those staying at the cabins and tents here. So stay, it's worth it for access to this most atmospheric of drinking dens. But don't worry, there are other pubs on this paddle, which launches just down a long leafy lane from Fforest's Farm 200-acre site.

It's here, a ten-minute drive east of Cardigan, that you'll find Heritage Canoes' base beside the River Teifi. It's called 'Wales' most untouched river', which is easy to believe when paddling here along the thickly wooded tidal gorge. Peregrine falcons zip from steep banks, and kingfishers dart above slow-moving water busy with salmon, sewin (sea trout) and otters. Heritage's two-hour trips are a fantastic experience, using Canadian-style canoes to explore the fern-fronded gulley, paddling upstream to Cilgerran, and back. The base is in woods at the Welsh Wildlife Centre and Teifi Marshes Nature Reserve (*welshwildlife.org/visit/welsh-wildlife-centre-teifi-marshes*), with a car park, a contemporary visitors' centre with a cafe and footpaths interspersed with bird hides.

I joined a trip with my children, with a fun and informative guide, Bryan Smith, who led the group along a 5.6km (3.5 miles) route that was dramatic in both scenery and experience – there

OPPOSITE: The bridge across the River Teifi in Cardigan.

BELOW: Heritage Canoes runs guided trips on the river.

44 RIVER TEIFI

CLOCKWISE FROM TOP LEFT: Seabass at The Ferry Inn, St Dogmael's; the cosy Y Bwthyn pub at the Fforest site; Mwnt beach; a sunny deck at the Fforest glamping site.

was some mild capsizing involved. After a relaxed start, a section of strong but shallow flow compelled the group to scramble onto the banks and follow an overgrown footpath for a few minutes while the guide towed all our rafted canoes on foot. Then, just before Cilgerran, we attempted to fight our way up some small but powerful rapids. One by one we paddled our canoes as furiously as we could, but were spun backwards, sideways and even, in the case of one poor woman with her son, upside down. We repeatedly took a turn, and repeatedly skidded to the back of the queue like it was some *Gladiators* challenge. But beauty was all around and it was hilarious – even those who capsized took their soaking in good spirits. You will probably have more luck. We made it to Cilgerran, where a 13th-century castle towers above the river. On our return, we hit the **Fforest Inn**.

Those using their own or hire kit could instead pull in at Cilgerran to visit its small, traditional and heartwarming pubs: the **Cardiff Arms**, serving Felinfoel Double Dragon ale and with a coracle hung on the exterior, and the **Mason's Arms**, also known as **The Rampin**, with an old kitchen range fire. You could also put in here to start your own adventure, as there's a car park with river access.

Heading west, you'll pass through the Teifi Marshes Nature Reserve, then the river widens and can become windy as you arrive into colourful Cardigan. Pull in and moor up for the **Albion Aberteifi**, Fforest's hip, waterside hotel. It has a sleek little cocktail bar and an outdoor courtyard beer garden with river views. On the opposite bank, **PizzaTipi** is another of its ventures, serving wood-fired pizzas in a huge venue with a festival feel, and with a little pub, **Tafarn Smwglin**, at its heart. The days when dozens of smwglin (tiny, secret, unlicensed 19th-century alehouses) filled the town's alleys have gone, but there's something of their hidden away atmosphere still here. Fforest's riverside pub, the **Crown Inn** is identifiable thanks to its bright red door.

Continue paddling towards the sea for another 1.5km (1 mile) and you'll come to the captivating village of St Dogmaels on the estuary, with its ruined abbey.

There's space to park, if you intend to leave one car at the end of the paddle, but more to the point there's **The Ferry Inn**, a wonderful low-key pub whose deck has glorious estuary views over waders, migratory birds and paddlers. The excellent

restaurant serves a mean seabass with roast potatoes. If the tide allows, you could continue a little further into the estuary to the beaches of Patch and Poppit Sands, but do return to the pub for sunset at the end of the world.

▸ Details

Join a two-hour tour to Cilgerran with Heritage Canoes (*heritagecanoes.squarespace.com*). Other operators run trips and offer hire along this stretch of the Teifi, including Adventure Beyond (*adventurebeyond.co.uk/activities-list/stand-up-paddle-boarding*) and SUP Cilgerran (*facebook.com/SUPCilgerran*). See the Cardigan Bay website (*cardigan-bay.com/canoe-along-the-river-teifi*) for route information. For the pubs, see (*facebook.com/p/Cardiff-Arms-Cilgerran*), (*albionaberteifi.co.uk*), (*coldatnight.co.uk/tafarn-smwglin*), (*albionaberteifi.co.uk/yr-odyn*), (*theferryinn.co.uk*), and for food, see (*pizzatipi.co.uk*).

▸ Make a weekend of it

Fforest Farm is a genre-defining glamping site, one of the first to make a name for itself when the trend took off in the mid-2000s. There's a range of accommodation, from geodesic domes with their own Japanese-style 'bathhouses' with deep wooden baths, to a farmhouse. A second, smaller site, Fforest Beach, at Manorafan, is a 15-minute walk from Penbryn beach, with log cabins and geodesic domes (*coldatnight.co.uk/manorafon-coast*). The Albion Aberteifi (*coldatnight.co.uk/fforest-town*) is an adults-only hotel with cool rooms styled like captains' cabins with Welsh blankets, and five self-catering Granary Lofts that do take families. The Welsh Wildlife Centre has a self-catering holiday rental on its site, Oak Tree Cottage, sleeping four (*welshwildlife.org/visit/welsh-wildlife-centre-teifi-marshes/oak-tree-cottage*).

Near here, Mwnt beach is unmissable, perfect for swimming, while Cwm Yr Eglwys is popular for dinghy sailing.

▸ Alternative route

Explore New Quay Bay by hiring paddleboards or kayaks from Cardigan Bay Watersports (*cardiganbaywatersports.org.uk*), then exploring quaint New Quay for seafood, cute shops and traditional pubs including **The Llwyngwair Arms** (*facebook.com/TafarnyLlwyn*).

OPPOSITE: Seats outside The Albion hotel and pub in Cardigan.

BELOW: Getting the canoes over the rapids on a Heritage Canoes tour.

Wales/Herefordshire

45　River Wye: The 100-mile pub crawl

- 160km (100 miles)
- Adventure, freedom, rural
- River
- One way
- No licence needed

The Wye is one of the UK's most rhapsodised rivers. Navigable pretty much for its full, 160km (100 mile) length, it cleaves a path between Wales and England for much of the way, from its Welsh Cambrian mountain source at Plynlimon through pretty Herefordshire and picture-perfect towns such as Hay-on-Wye, Ross-on-Wye and Monmouth. It is possible, and quite popular, to paddle the whole thing, taking your time, camping or staying in pubs along the way. Lovely villages, deep ravines and hills 'clad in one green hue' as Wordsworth put it are linked on its course until dissipation into the River Severn at Chepstow. There are pubs galore along the way.

In practice, the section above Hay-on-Wye is often too low to paddle, except in winter, so it's the stretch downriver from there that is most commonly explored.

Few rivers have so many canoe and kayak operators offering adventures along their length, and things can get a little competitive. There are dozens of different organised excursions or

multi-day holidays to choose from. But the opportunity for a self-led journey of several days, stopping at pubs and beauty spots, is a true pursuit of freedom and exhilaration.

You could argue that the Wye is potentially one gigantic pub crawl (but remember paddling under the influence is a no-no, so have your drinks at the end of each day). It's a marvellous thing to take days over it, booking with an operator who can handle the logistics, each day's distances and lazy stops to camp, walk, spot birdlife, wild boar, deer and otters, and enjoy the excellent waterside pubs that have supplicated boaters for centuries.

From Hay-on-Wye, travelling 8.9km (5.5 miles) downriver you come to the **Boat Inn**, serving local ales with a rural beer garden looking across to fields. Located between Hay and Witney, the Black Mountains and Radnorshire Hills shape the pub's surroundings.

Hoarwithy has a very nice campsite, and a beach landing. The village is home to the **New Harp Inn**, a smart grey number with a beer garden (not on the water).

Ross-on-Wye is a superb little town of quirky shops, and home to **The Hope and Anchor**. This pub is quite modernised inside, and the grass out the front is often busy with dogs, kids and drinkers.

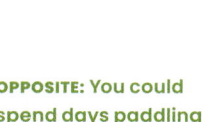

OPPOSITE: You could spend days paddling the River Wye, stopping at pubs along the way (photo: iStock).

BELOW: Canoeists on the River Wye (photo: iStock).

CLOCKWISE FROM TOP LEFT: Crossing the bridge from Penalt to The Boat Inn (photo: Nicki Liddiard); Hay-on-Wye in autumn (photo: iStock); picture postcard Ross-on-Wye (photo: iStock).

As a place to pull in for a pint it makes a fine stop, with a snack hut outside, and accommodation.

The White Lion at Wilton, five minutes downriver from Ross-on-Wye, has more character. Its benches are a Scampi Fry's toss from the water.

Symonds Yat comes next, with two glorious pubs, **Ye Old Ferrie Inn** and the **Saracen's Head Inn**, as covered on pages 230 to 232.

Pass through delightful Monmouth, where a lack of riverside hostelries is counterbalanced by a diverting high street full of cool cafes and bookshops, as well as a few pubs including **The Castle** (facebook.com/thecastleinnmonmouth), offering Cwtch and Butty Bach on tap.

The Boat Inn at Penallt, opposite Redbrook is a characterful stop. It's set in a fern-filled, waterfall-riddled nook that is pretty and atmospheric, with seats undercover on the other side of a narrow lane, looking over the river.

Then a little inland, but worth the effort, is the **Lion Inn** in Trellech, a good old-fashioned venue with a sign out front proclaiming it a 'man creche'. It has a rental cottage and B&B, regular live folk music and a summer beer festival.

Tintern has some great pubs, including the waterside **The Anchor**, dating back to the 12th century. The abbey and wooded hills rising steeply behind it make for a spectacular backdrop.

A final fling is in Chepstow, at **The Boat Inn**, a quaint spot the colour of clotted cream, with beams and flagstone floors.

▶ Details

Paddle UK's webpage for the Wye (*gopaddling.info/rivers/river-wye*) links to a series of detailed river guides for different stretches, with launch points, campsites and other places of interest. There's more info from the regional tourist board (*visitherefordshire.co.uk/see-do/get-active/canoeing-sup*).

Many operators run paddle trips along the route. These include Hereford Canoes (*herefordcanoehire.com*); Monmouth Canoe Hire (*monmouthcanoe.co.uk*), whose trips stop at the Ye Old Ferrie Inn (YOFI) for lunch; and Wye Canoes (*wyecanoes.com*) which arranges multi-day self-led trips along the whole 160km (100 miles) as well as rental, or a full day trip to Symonds Yat West from Ross-on-Wye. Herefordshire Canoe Hire is based at Tresseck Campsite in Hoarwithy; Hereford Kayak and Canoe Hire

BELOW: The River Wye from Symonds Yat.

(*herefordkayakcanoe.co.uk*) has bases at Hereford and Byecross. For the pubs, see (*boatinn-whitney.co.uk*), (*thenewharpinn.co.uk*), (*thehopeandanchor.co.uk*), (*whitelionross.com*), (*yeoldferrieinn.com*), (*saracensheadinn.co.uk*), (*facebook.com/thecastleinnmonmouth*), (*theboatinnpenalt.co.uk*), (*lioninn.co.uk*), (*theanchortintern.co.uk*) and (*theboatinnchepstow.co.uk*).

❱ Make a weekend of it

Book with one of the operators offering multi-day trips for a longer paddle and camping adventure, such as Wye Canoes. For a good stay before setting off from Hay-on-Wye, nearby glamping and cottages are available at Drovers Rest farm (*droversrest.co.uk*) – inspired by the vineyards of the South African owners' home country, it has great food, drinks and animals to pet. Similar but smarter is Cynefin Retreats (*cynefinretreats.com*), for bodacious, curvaceous cabins.

In Ross on Wye, The Hope and Anchor (*thehopeandanchor.co.uk*) has 12 neat bedrooms, or there's the luxurious riverside country mansion hotel Bridge House (*bridgehouserossonwye.co.uk*), with nine rooms. Ye Old Ferrie Inn (*yeoldferrieinn.com*) has lovely rooms in Symonds Yat. At the far end, in Tintern, try The Wild Hare (*thewildharetintern.co.uk*), a chic pub with rooms.

OPPOSITE: The River Wye heading into Herefordshire (photo: iStock).

BELOW: A footbridge over the River Wye downriver from Symonds Yat.

Wales / Herefordshire

46 River Wye: Symonds Yat and Ye Old Ferrie Inn

- 1.6km (1 mile)
- Rural, easy, fun
- River
- Out and back
- Licence needed

'It should really be called Ye *Very* Old Ferrie Inn,' jokes landlord Jamie Hicks when we meet at his fine waterside hostelry in Herefordshire's Symonds Yat. 'After all, it was established in 1473.'

Bags of personality is a description that could be applied to both the venue and the man, whose family have lived in the area for five generations. There are dozens of pubs on the Wye, but Jamie has made his place one of the favourites.

Downstairs, a long dining room with sanded farmhouse tables has windows along one side with pretty views of the river. Green walls display old black and white photos of the pub, showing great hay bales out front, and the old veranda that once ran around the exterior. This has essentially been revived in modern form, with an oak framed extension creating a kind of loggia. It's built on stilts to avoid a repeat of the disastrous flood that wrecked the place in February 2020 during Storm Dennis, when the pub benches washed up as far away as Portishead.

As well as the likes of slow-cooked Herefordshire lamb shoulder, venison cottage pie and veggie curry, you can also get supplies to go, including Wye Gin, local Franks biscuits, plus cans of Starting Gate cocktails. Upstairs, cosy bedrooms are supplied with binoculars for tracking the peregrine falcons that zip from the cliffs across the water, and outside, a long terrace beer garden stretches down towards Symonds Yat, always filled with a happy crowd at the merest suggestion of sunshine.

Plenty of paddlers doing longer routes along the river call in here, but the pub also has its own rental outlet, YOFI Paddlesports, that's perfect for dipping your toe in for an hour or two. Sturdy green Canadian-style canoes or SUPs can be rented by the hour, but you can also book lessons and longer adventures.

It was a particularly powerful river the spring week when I went out, torrential rain had meant all river trips were off for a week. When we did go out, paddling upstream in a rafted canoe with my kids, the flow was so powerful we barely moved.

But then, the sun exploded the landscape into a sparkling wooded heaven and the tremendous flow eased enough for us to set out, skirting a weeping willow, circumnavigating a small island for practice then pushing upstream.

The drama of the landscape outweighs its quaintness – sheer cliffs rise above the winding river and up on the hillside is the red villa made famous by the Netflix show *Sex Education*.

YOFI doesn't offer a pick-up service, so heading up against the current then back to the pub again is the only direction allowed. We paddled up to St Dubricius church then back to the YOFI to hit

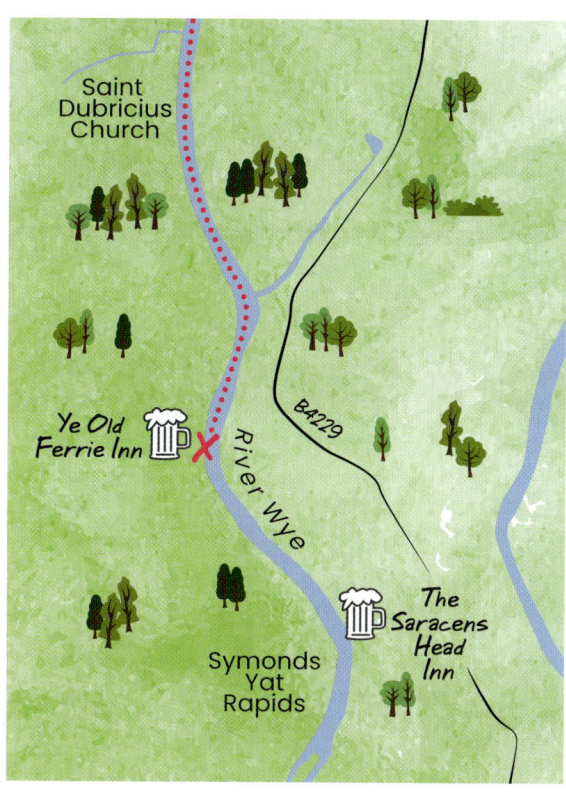

OPPOSITE: Canoes for rent outside Ye Old Ferrie Inn.

the horsebox bar in the beer garden for the Wye Valley Brewery's Butty Bach. A short but satisfying canoe that's a great intro to this beloved paddlers' river.

For those with their own gear, there's a put-in about a kilometre further up the road, upstream from the pub. There's no public river access from the pub itself, though boaters are welcome to stop off as customers.

▶ Alternative route

A little way downriver at the foot of the deep wooded gorge at Symonds Yat East is the **Saracen's Head Inn** (*saracensheadinn.co.uk*), centuries old, with good food and drink, as well as outdoor seating looking out to the hand-pulled ferry that crosses the water. Thought to have run since Roman times, the ferry is one of only two that remain. In the 1800s, some 25 ferries ran between Chepstow and Ross-on-Wye.

Most casual paddlers will not want to hit them but 800m (0.5 miles) down from YOFI is Symonds Yat Rapid, owned by Paddle UK (*gopaddling.info/rivers/river-wye*) and run by volunteers, it has a course laid out for whitewater paddlers to practise. You could portage around. Next stop is Monmouth (no waterside pubs, but good ones in town). Or upriver from YOFI are Coppett Hill, Kerne Bridge and Goodrich Castle, then gorgeous Ross-on-Wye.

ABOVE: The Monmouthshire and Brecon Canal has been voted the country's prettiest canal (photo: iStock).

▶ Details

Hire canoes, paddleboards, and giant SUPs, and book lessons and tours from YOFI (*yeoldferrieinn.com*). They offer 'early-bird' and 'night owl' paddles, when you might see otters, as well as a half-day excursion from Kerne Bridge down to YOFI.

For information on paddling the River Wye, see (*gopaddling.info/rivers/river-wye*) and on the area, see (*forestryengland.uk/symonds-yat-rock*).

▶ Make a weekend of it

Ye Old Ferrie Inn (*yeoldferrieinn.com*) has six comfortable rooms and does a great breakfast. The Saracen's Head (*saracensheadinn.co.uk*) has B&B rooms and a four-bedroom cottage, The Weir House. Be sure to hike up to Symonds Yat rock to survey the gorgeous curve of the river for views stretching an unbelievable distance.

More great paddles in Wales

MONMOUTHSHIRE AND BRECON CANAL

In the Brecon Beacons/Bannau Brycheiniog national park, hire kayaks, SUPs or even cycle boats (like a sleek pedalo) and electric self-drive motorboats from Beacon Park Day Boats (*beaconparkdayboats.co.uk*). Take off along the Monmouthshire and Brecon canal under overhanging oaks and with views of the Usk Valley, of Table Mountain and Crickhowell. Head north and you might make it to the **Coach and Horses** (*coachandhorsesllangynidr.com*), which has benches set out on the grass right by the canal.

LLYN PADARN, SNOWDONIA

The 3.2km (2 mile) long glacial Llyn Padarn cuts a slash through the rugged mountains of Snowdonia on the edge of the Eryri National Park. Along its southern shore, the busy outdoorsy town of

BELOW: Port Eynon beach on the Gower Peninsula (photo: iStock).

Llanberis caters to the region's adventurers with cafes, shops and hostelries such as **The Heights** (*theheightsllanberis.co.uk*), a bunkhouse and pub 100m (330ft) from the water's edge. Hire kit and book lessons from Snowdonia Watersports (*snowdoniawatersports.com*). Soak up views of a photogenic lone tree, of Dolbadarn Castle and the Glyn Rhonwy slate quarries, and look out for rare species found here, including arctic char and floating water-plantain. There are several public car parks near the shore. See (*snowdonia.gov.wales*).

THE GOWER PENINSULA

With some of Wales best beaches, the Gower, west of Swansea, is a wonderful area for a holiday, with a fantastic coastal path linking beauty spots such as Three Cliffs Bay, Rhosillli Bay and Oxwich beach. At its most southerly point, Port Eynon, **The Ship Inn** (*shipinngower.co.uk*) has been dramatically revamped in recent years to pay stylish respect to the town's seafaring history, with wood panelling and nautical features. Port Eynon was such a smugglers' hotspot, even its church was once a den of iniquity, but its most notorious outlaw, John Lucas, wasn't all bad – he was a Robin Hood type who shared his spoils with the locals. There's a YHA (*yha.org.uk*) right on the beach, its adjoining activity centre (*goweractivitycentres.co.uk*) offers watersports including SUP and kayaking.

BELOW: Houses line the steep banks of the Wye near Symonds Yat.

Northern Ireland

47 The Causeway Coast: Ballycastle and the Giant's Causeway

- 1.6 to 8km (1 to 5 miles)
- Dramatic, beach, craic
- Sea
- Out and back
- No licence needed

On the north-east coast of **Northern Ireland** in County Antrim, the Causeway Coast is the region's most impressive and spectacular landscape. Here, with a great flat sweep of sand, and cliffs so high and sheer Red Bull has hosted cliff diving events on them, Ballycastle offers variety in spades. Not only is there a gorgeous beach, with views all the way across to the Kintyre peninsula in Scotland, but it's an interesting stepping off point for further adventures. A ferry departs from here for Rathlin island, an untouched beauty spot for hiking and birdwatching. However, you don't have to voyage so far for your hit of nature's wonder.

Book a trip with Coastal Connections Causeway Coast Kayaking Tours. Depart from Ballycastle harbour, which featured as one of the Iron Islands in *Game of Thrones*. Some tours take you past Northern Ireland's primary natural attraction, the Giant's Causeway. Once you've had your fill of interesting rock formations and of the lively harbour and beach, the closest drinking spots are the **Harbour Bar** on the seafront, and the **Angler's Arms**, both small, old-school, and traditional. The place to stick around for the evening though is **O'Connors Bar**, up the road on Ann Street, with

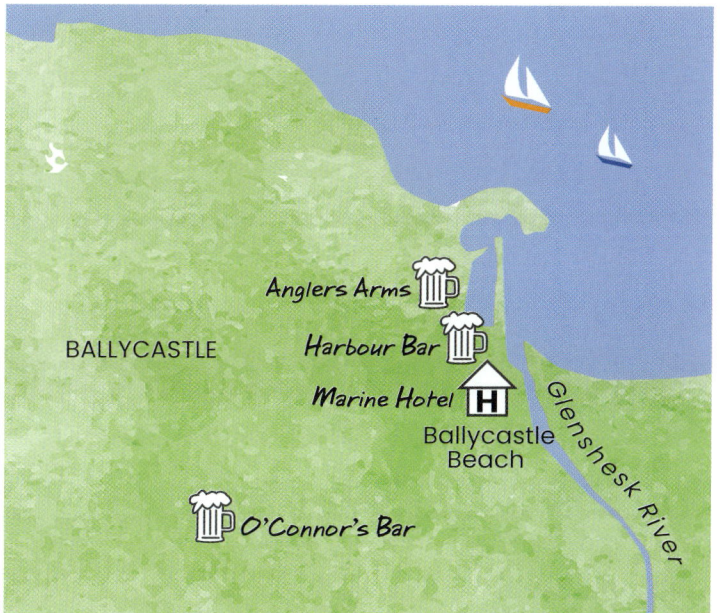

proper Irish music played live and artfully presented plates of food. Celebs including *Game of Thrones* actors and Jamie Dornan have been spotted there.

You might want to get your chips (and possibly some monkfish scampi) from Morton's though, a takeaway place at the harbour that's the tastiest around. The Marine Hotel has a swish bistro if you want something posher.

▶ Details

Book tours or hire with Coastal Connections Causeway Coast Kayaking Tours (*causewaycoastkayakingtours.com*). Far and Wild (*farandwild.org*) runs interesting tours along this coast, including moonlit tours and those by giant 'dragon' SUPs. For info, see (*discovernorthernireland.com*) and (*visitcausewaycoastandglens.com*). For the pubs, see (*oconnorsbar.ie*), (*marinehotelballycastle.com*), and others can be found on Facebook.

▶ Make a weekend of it

Stay in Ballycastle at smart eco hotel the Salt House (*thesalthousehotel.com*), which has outdoor seaweed baths and hot tubs and a panoramic sauna, or at Trench Farm (*trenchfarm.com*), which has a cottage, camping pitches… and alpacas.

OPPOSITE: The basalt rock formations of the Giant's Causeway (photo: iStock).

More great paddles in Northern Ireland

CUSHENDALL AND CUSHENDUN

Independent, experienced paddlers can bring their kit down to an interesting slash of coastline between the villages of Cushendall and Cushendun, which both have pretty pale sand beaches. Look out for offshore breezes created where the Glens of Antrim run down to the sea, and for the swell as you dip around the rocks. To the south, Glenarm is a pebble and sand beach with views of headlands and hills. Causeway Coast Kayak Tours (*causewaycoastkayakingtours.com*) runs trips in the area, as does Sea Kayak Ulster (*seakayakulster.com*), which recommends these beaches on account of the post-paddle pint opportunities in the villages. The pubs of Cushendall include the **Lurig Bar** (*mcnaughtonguestrooms.com*) which also has bedrooms, or **Johnny Joes** (*facebook.com/johnnyjoescushendall*) which, despite being bright pink, is traditional, and hosts live music.

BELOW: Cushendun on the Causeway Coast (photo: iStock).

OPPOSITE: The Carrick-a-Rede Rope Bridge in Ballintoy, County Antrim (photo: iStock).

ABOVE: Kayakers on the beach below the Carrick-a-Rede bridge (photo: iStock).

DERRY/LONDONDERRY

Experience the calm of 'the blue way' through the city of Derry on a SUP tour with Far and Wild (*farandwild.org/city-paddle-boards*). The tidal estuary of the Foyle River (Feabhail) runs through the city and down to the Atlantic to the north; whether you go up or downstream depends on the tide, but these two-hour trips from a base in St Colum Park will reveal nature and peace of an urban, but wide open river. The tour ends with tacos at **Pyke n' Pommes** (*pykenpommes.ie*), a casual but tasty restaurant, which has a big waterside beer terrace for food and drinks.

BALLINTOY AND THE CAUSEWAY COAST

Paddle beneath the spectacular Carrick-a-Rede suspension bridge, strung between rocks 30m (100ft) up by salmon fishermen some 250 years ago, then out to Elephant Rock or to see the sunset from the water – all options on a tour from Ballintoy. Causeway Coast Kayaking Tours (*causewaycoastkayakingtours.com*) offers these and more from the harbour of the north coastal town, which lies west along the coast from Ballycastle. Then return to the **Carrick-a-Rede Bar** (*carrickaredebar.co.uk*) on Main Street, which hosts live music every Saturday.